EDUCATION SINCE UHURU
THE SCHOOLS OF KENYA

# Education Since Uhuru

# The Schools of Kenya

By ERNEST STABLER

WESLEYAN UNIVERSITY PRESS
*Middletown, Connecticut*

Copyright © 1969 by Wesleyan University

LA
1561
.S7

Library of Congress Catalog Card Number: 70-82539
Manufactured in the United States of America

FIRST EDITION

To I, M, and D

Affairs are now soul size.
—Christopher Fry, *A Sleep of Prisoners*

## Contents

| | |
|---|---|
| *Preface* | xiii |
| *A Note on Currencies* | xv |
| *Acknowledgements* | xvii |
| *Introduction: Land and People* | xix |

### PART ONE. BEFORE AND AFTER UHURU

*Chapter*

ONE *The Colonial Legacy*     3
    Trusteeship and Adaptation
    Attack on a Vicious Circle
    The Tempo Quickens

### PART TWO. PRIMARY EDUCATION

TWO *Primary Schools: Teachers and Children*     25

THREE *The New Primary Approach*     35
    English Medium and Activity Methods
    *Peak* and *New Peak*
    Growth and Acceptance
    Analysis and Evaluation
    Research and Development

FOUR *The Education of Primary Teachers: Kagumo College*     58
    Kagumo College
    Student Life
    Expatriate and African Staff
    A Crowded Curriculum
    Teaching Practice
    Model Schools and Teacher Upgrading

PART THREE. SECONDARY EDUCATION

*Chapter*

FIVE *Schools in Transition*   77
    The Rule of Cambridge
    Curriculum Change
    *Harambee*
    Secondary Expansion
    Staffing
    Desegregation

SIX *A Former European School: Kenya High*   87
    Monument and Memorial
    Standards and Service
    A Secure Society
    The Strains of Integration

SEVEN *An African School: Alliance*   103
    Strong to Serve
    A Complex Society
    A Climate for Learning
    Headmaster and Staff
    Prefects and the Sixth Form
    A Lighthouse Role?

EIGHT *A Pilot School: Chavakali*   119
    Maragoli Country
    A Quaker Founding
    Agriculture and Industrial Arts
    Chavakali in 1968
    Chavakali's Dilemmas

NINE *The Education of Secondary Teachers:*
    *Kenya Science Teachers College*   137
    A Model of External Aid
    Agents of Change
    Staff and Counterparts
    The Three-Year Course
    The Students
    Impact

PART FOUR. THE WAY AHEAD

TEN *Pressures, Constraints, and New Directions*     159
    The Population Problem
    Political and Social Pressures
    Economic Restraints
    Adaptation, African Style

*Selected Bibliography*     177
    Books and Articles
    Committee, Commission, and Conference Reports
    Kenya Government Documents
        MINISTRY OF AGRICULTURE
        MINISTRY OF ECONOMIC PLANNING AND
           DEVELOPMENT
        MINISTRY OF EDUCATION
        MINISTRY OF INFORMATION

# *Preface*

RUNNING through this book is my belief that it is possible to reveal the educational condition of a new and developing country through a series of profiles of several of its schools and colleges. I recognize of course that every school is unique and that a set of verbal photographs provides concrete and particular evidence rather than generalizations, but as representative examples it may contribute to an understanding of the whole educational enterprise. Through visits and interviews I have attempted to interpret each school and college as accurately as possible and to capture some of the spirit of its inner life.

In the years following Uhuru (Independence), which was won in 1963, great changes have come to education in Kenya. And for the chronicler these changes create a dilemma; on the one hand they deserve to be recorded, yet change is so rapid that any interpretation or analysis soon needs to be revised. One example may suffice: the profiles were written in 1967 and 1968 and for all kinds of reasons—the arrival of a new headmaster, turnover of staff, change in admissions policy, or introduction of new courses—the schools are now rather different. But the general *direction* of change may remain the same, unless (as is quite possible) Kenya makes a major alteration in her education priorities.

An introductory chapter considers educational policy and practice during the colonial period, the portraits of schools occupy the central portion of the book, and a final chapter draws implications and, within the context of a variety of constraints and pressures, discusses the options available to a new nation within the first decade of Independence. It is my hope that the cumulative effect will illumine an African society in a period of transition.

E.S.

*November, 1968*

## *A Note on Currencies*

THROUGHOUT the book Kenyan and American currencies are used, and costs are shown in the appropriate context. There are twenty shillings in a Kenya pound (20/ = £1); and seven shillings are equivalent to an American dollar.

# Acknowledgements

I RECALL with affection the officials and headmasters, teachers and students who helped me to shape the content of this book. In particular, I wish to thank James Njoroge, Permanent Secretary of the Ministry of Education, and Kyale Mwendwa, Chief Education Officer, for their permission to visit schools and colleges and for their friendly assistance. The views expressed throughout the book are, of course, my own and are in no way intended to be an expression of official policy.

The Ford Foundation assisted me in revisiting Kenya in the summers of 1967 and 1968, and to Francis Sutton, formerly the Representative of the Foundation in Nairobi, I am deeply grateful. For many courtesies I wish to thank the Nairobi staff of the Foundation and in particular, Jack Robin, Mary Ann Wiesner, and George and Kathleen Reynolds.

My warm thanks go also to these men and women whose present and former affiliations are shown in parentheses: Alexander Getao (Kagumo); Laurence Campbell and Fred Dollimore (Alliance); Adrienne Leevers (Kenya High); Thomas Howes, David Hunter, Robert Maxwell, and Philip Towle (Chavakali); Olov Bergman, Lars Bjorkman, and Olle Osterling (Kenya Science Teachers College); Roger Carter (Ministry of Education) and Matthew Mwenesi (Ministry of Labour).

Arnold Curtis, a member of the Inspectorate, gave generous help in the collection of material and has offered much valuable criticism.

And finally, I am indebted to Penny Apter, Nargis Keshavjee, and Angela Ogden for typing the manuscript.

## Introduction: Land and People

A LITTLE larger than France and a little smaller than Texas, Kenya straddles the equator on the eastern seaboard of Africa. From the hot and humid coastal strip the land rises through dry bush country to savannah grasslands and fertile and well-watered highlands. The Great Rift Valley slices Kenya in two, and beyond its western rim the land slopes down to Lake Victoria and the Uganda border. Almost the entire northern half of the country is arid and sparsely populated by nomadic tribesmen. Altitude largely determines climate and highland areas above 5,000 feet are temperate throughout the year.

The 1970 estimate for Kenya's population is 10,850,000. The overwhelming majority are Africans who represent four different ethnic groups (Bantu, Nilotic, Nilo-Hamitic, and Hamitic) and some fifty tribes. The term "Asian" is used to refer to some quarter of a million of the population whose origins are chiefly India and Pakistan. It was this group that until very recently supplied Kenya with clerks and artisans, dominated the retail trade, and played an important role in the leadership of commerce and industry. Immigration after the two World Wars swelled the European population, and by 1960 it numbered 70,000, the majority of whom were of British origin. Kenyanization policies, both actual and presumed, particularly in agriculture, have accounted for a reduction of some 40 per cent of the European group.

Agriculture is the chief industry and three-quarters of all Kenya families are farmers or herdsmen. Reforms in land tenure including the consolidation of scattered fragments into compact small holdings, and the registration of freehold ownership have led to marked increases in production. Settlement schemes have placed African farmers on land formerly owned by Europeans and known as the White Highlands. Coffee, tea, and sisal are the chief cash crops.

But facts and statistics cannot give anything of the "feel" of an emerging country, and a sense of contrasts and tensions that permeate its life. In Nairobi, the capital, homeless families may be cooking over open fires only a few steps away from a supermarket, and up country a barefoot woman who carries a water pitcher on her head may have a college-educated son who drives a Mercedes. In one issue (July 14, 1967) selected at random the *East African Standard* (Nairobi) chronicled these several events:

> Mr. Oginga Odinga, Leader of the Opposition, said in Parliament, "We oppose family planning and we don't even want to hear of family planning in Kenya. At the moment the Black man provides the tiniest population in the world and yet he lives on a vast continent; everyone knows that Kenya is empty. In Africa we should encourage people to live a healthy, decent life and to produce as many children as they can."
>
> A member of Parliament alleged that his brother had died after an accident because there had been no doctor available to treat him on arrival at the hospital in Nakuru—a town of 60,000.
>
> The Donovan Maule Repertory Theatre in Nairobi will complete its run of Sheridan's *The Rivals* and open next week with a comedy from London's West End, *There's a Girl in My Soup*.
>
> A man carrying a leopard skin in the streets and unable to produce a Game Department license was brought before a Magistrate.
>
> The Welsh Society of Kenya announced it would hold a social evening at the Equator Inn. Bar service would be available.
>
> A member of the Legislative Assembly who had been detained for several weeks without trial under the Public Security Act has been released.

*Introduction: Land and People* / xxi

Minimum wages were announced: 175/ per month for male and 140/ for female workers in Nairobi; 160/ for males elsewhere in Kenya.

TV programs during the week-end included *I Spy, Flintstones* and *My Favorite Martian.*

When settlers began arriving in Kenya soon after the turn of the twentieth century they found a sparsely settled and, by European standards, a primitive population. In a work that combined a biography of Lord Delamere, one of Kenya's earliest settlers and certainly its most remarkable, and a history of white settlement, Elspeth Huxley reveals the early settler's outlook towards the African:

> The land set aside for lease to settlers was (contrary to much that has been said and written) empty, or almost empty, of human beings. It lay there as nature made it, uncultivated, untouched, dormant—a challenge to the pioneer. The native population was not only sparse but exceedingly primitive. The various tribes had never grouped themselves into strong and stable units under powerful chiefs, as in Buganda, and even more, in West Africa; for the most part they were nomadic or practised shifting cultivation, their tools wooden digging sticks, their weapons spears and arrows, their faith animistic, and their beasts of burden their womenfolk. They knew nothing of the arts of writing, architecture, or mechanics, they were clad in skins and feathers, they were ignorant of such simple devices as the plough, the coin, the pump, the loom or the wheel.[1]

Sixty years later, at midnight on December 12, 1963, as the Union Jack was furled and the red, green, and black of Kenya was raised to mark the beginning of Independence, Jomo Kenyatta, the son of one of those primitive men, became the Prime Minister, and later the President of Kenya. In the meantime, during the period of colonial rule, Kenya had experienced remarkable changes. Modern methods of farming were introduced to the Kenya Highlands; a public administration created a tax structure and a network of government services;

---

[1] Elspeth Huxley, *White Man's Country: Lord Delamere and the Making of Kenya* (London: Chatto and Windus, 2nd ed. 1953), p. vi.

African, Asian, and European children were sent to school, African churches had grown out of Christian missions, and underlying the relationships among men of different colors and beliefs was the rule of law.

These were far-reaching achievements for a period of six decades, but by other criteria Kenya is a very underdeveloped country, and at Independence she faced a mountainous set of problems. Her annual per capita income in 1964 was only slightly over £30, and 60 per cent of African men were engaged in subsistence farming. She had few natural resources other than land, and the immediate prospects for an agrarian revolution were not bright. The rate of population growth was high, 3 per cent a year, and nearly half of the population was under fifteen years of age. Problems in education were particularly acute. A 1964 survey of high-level manpower revealed how few Africans there were in the professions: thirty-six doctors, twenty electrical engineers, seventeen university teachers, and seven economists. And along with the need to train middle- and high-level manpower there lay the question of how the schools should be used as instruments of national planning.

## *Uhuru and After* [2]

WITHIN a month of Independence the Minister of Education appointed a commission under the chairmanship of Professor S. H. Ominde to survey the existing educational resources and advise the new Government in the formulation and implementation of policy. The members of the Commission (ten of the fourteen were Africans) were acutely aware of the differences that separated them from colonial committees on education. Never before had an inquiry been made into the whole of education in Kenya. Earlier committees had never regarded education as one system and had assumed that the several communities would remain long, if not forever, separate, and the

---

[2] This section borrows freely from the author's Introduction to the *Ministry of Education Annual Summary* (Nairobi: Government Printer, 1965).

education provided for each should correspond to the social and occupational role its members could be expected to play in national life. With Independence a nation was born and ahead lay the task of bringing not only the different racial groups but the various tribes into some kind of unity. The notion of *harambee* (working together) was a new idea, a break with the colonial past, and the commission knew that education must now serve as an instrument in developing a sense of national unity.

Previous committees of inquiry had assumed that education would be supported largely by Christian missions and churches. The first recommendation of the Beecher Committee of 1949 urged the Government "to work with and through those voluntary agencies which have the teaching of Christian principles as part of their intention." Fifteen years later the Ominde Commission felt that the practice of leaving the management of maintained primary schools in the hands of the missions had "outlived its usefulness" and was no longer appropriate in a secular state. Primary education should, henceforth, be managed by public not religious authorities.

While the Commission was at work, the *Development Plan 1964–70*, the survey *High Level Manpower Requirements and Resources in Kenya 1964–70*, and *African Socialism and its Application to Planning in Kenya* were all published. And with them a new principle appeared: education and national development must form a partnership. Economic growth can be speeded up if education produces the middle- and high-level manpower which a developing country needs so desperately. The change was twofold: never before had education been regarded as the seed of economic development. Schools had hitherto been regarded more as social than economic institutions and their function was to train individuals for their appropriate place in society. Now education was to be considered as a service to the state through the production of engineers and teachers, doctors and agronomists, mechanics and secretaries, and all the other skilled people in short supply. But it was not just a matter of training manpower, it must be *African* manpower, and the expansion of secondary, technical, and higher education must be achieved by increasing African enrollments. *African Socialism* made this quite clear:

> At Kenya's stage of development, education is much more an economic than a social service. It is our principal means for relieving the shortage of domestic skilled manpower and equalizing economic opportunities among all citizens. . . . The immediate objectives in education are to expand secondary level facilities as rapidly as teacher supply and recurrent cost implications permit. This is, of course, important to the training of manpower, the acceleration of Africanizaton and increasing the proportion of KPE candidates that can continue in education. . . . The plans for Nairobi University College must be fully integrated within the Government Development Plan if the University College is to contribute effectively in solving our manpower problem.[3]

Gradually, the context in which this manpower would be educated must also become African. Soon local teachers should replace expatriates, and the curriculum of the primary and secondary schools would, as the terms of reference given to the Commission put it, "appropriately express the aspirations and cultural values of an independent African country." Education in Kenya is in transition because society itself is under rapid change while Kenya decides which African strands in the pattern of culture it wants to strengthen, which European elements it will accept or reject, and whether components of both can be merged into a new and unique pattern. African culture is less in being than in becoming, as the search goes on for ways of combining the communal, protective, and spiritual traditions of the tribe, with the scientific, secular, and individualistic ethic of the West. This involves using the schools to create national unity and making education an agent for the shaping of a new society, while at the same time struggling to find the basic design and structure of that society.

---

[3] Sessional Paper No. 10, *African Socialism and its Application to Planning in Kenya* (Nairobi: Government Printer, 1965), p. 40.

PART ONE. BEFORE AND AFTER UHURU

[CHAPTER ONE]

## *The Colonial Legacy*

> No Native Tribes in the world have been subjected to such a forcing process as those of Kenya Colony. Nowhere has the whole system of civilization been dropped so suddenly and completely in the midst of savage races as here. In 1895 I crossed from Mombasa to the mainland in a dugout canoe and walked into the interior. Twenty-eight years later these infant races are shaking their rattles and talking politics! It is a situation that may well give pause to missionaries and officials alike, for it has within it the seeds of an unprecedented development or an appalling disaster.
>
> An American missionary quoted in<br>*Education in East Africa,* 1924

IN the years before Independence there were three significant turning points in the education of Africans. In the 1920's, soon after Kenya had officially been designated as a colony and protectorate, tensions began to develop among Africans, Indians, and the increasing number of Europeans who had settled in Kenya following World War I. The British Government intervened, clarified its policy toward the long-term welfare of the native population, and established the principles on which it would develop a colonial system of education. Some twenty-five years later when African primary schools were expanding rapidly the Government asked a committee chaired by Archdeacon L. J. Beecher to give its advice not only on the administration of primary education but on the larger question of the use of public funds for educating African children. Initially, the committee was restricted by its terms of reference to inquire into financial questions only, but later the range of inquiry was widened to include "the scope, content and methods of the African educational system." The "Beecher Report," *African Education in Kenya,* influenced both the pace of development and the quality of African education in the next ten years. And finally, in the five years before Independence there was an acceleration of the educational tempo when Africans increasingly secured places in secondary and higher education in preparation for their appointment to more responsible positions.

## Trusteeship and Adaptation

AFTER the first World War when European settlers were faced with a shortage of farm labor the first post-war governor, Sir Edward Northey, authorized government officials to "exercise every possible lawful influence to induce able-bodied natives to go into the labor field." Missionary leaders in Kenya and Britain protested this decision to allow government officers to act as recruiting agents for European farmers and asked the Imperial Government for some assurance of protection for Africans and for a clear and resolute policy directed to "the fostering of native life and institutions." At about the same time feeling was running high in Kenya between the Indian community and European settlers. In the first Legislative Council eleven members represented the Europeans and only two the Indian community although it outnumbered the Europeans by three to one. When a British government committee proposed to give political parity to the Indians the settlers raised a stormy protest, formed a vigilance committee, and began making plans to kidnap the Governor and set up a republic. The Imperial Government sensed the need for a statement of policy that would clarify the question as to whether the interests of the Africans or those of the immigrant races were to be paramount in Kenya. In July, 1923, the Colonial

## The Colonial Legacy / 5

Secretary issued a White Paper which put self-government by a minority race out of the question and prepared the way for new developments in the education of Africans:

> Primarily Kenya is an African territory, and His Majesty's Government think it necessary definitely to record their considered opinion that the interests of the African natives must be paramount, and that if and when, those interests and the interests of the immigrant races should conflict, the former should prevail. . . . His Majesty's Government cannot but regard the grant of responsible self-government as out of the question within any period of time which need now be taken into consideration. . . . As in the Uganda Protectorate, so in the Kenya Colony the principle of Trusteeship for the Natives no less than in the Mandated Territory of Tanganyika is unassailable.[1]

In developing an educational policy for Tropical Africa the British and colonial governments were deeply influenced by two studies of African education, usually referred to as the Phelps Stokes Reports, made by British and American educators and missionaries and one African in 1920-1921 and again in 1924. The chairman of the Commission, Jesse Jones, formerly of the Hampton Institute of Virginia, and his colleagues believed that the work of Hampton and Tuskegee with the American rural Negro could be applied to the African scene. The reports developed a philosophy of "adaptation" and argued that education "must be of a character to draw out the powers of the Native African and fit him to meet the specific problems and needs of his individual and community life." [2] Along with training in the three R's there should be a stress on health and hygiene, agriculture and gardening, industrial training and home economics. Religious values should permeate the atmosphere and teaching of the schools, and a partnership between the missions and colonial governments was the most

---

[1] Great Britain, White Paper entitled *Indians in Kenya* (1923, Cmd. 1922).

[2] *Education in East Africa* (New York: Phelps Stokes Fund, 1924), p. xvii.

effective way to administer primary education. The vernaculars should be recognized as the first language of instruction.

The education of Africans must also include the training of African leaders in agriculture, medicine, theology, and teaching. In 1924 there were only two colleges open to Africans south of the Sahara (Fourah Bay in Sierra Leone and Fort Hare in South Africa), and the number of secondary schools was negligible; in East Africa there was none. A few Africans had gone off to Europe and America for technical and professional training but in the future native leaders should have access to higher education at home.

The Phelps Stokes Reports were enthusiastically received in both Britain and the colonies, and the basic notions of the commission found their way into a second White Paper entitled *Educational Policy in British Tropical Africa.* It is a statement that reiterates the adaptation theme of Phelps Stokes and at the same time recommends the transfer of British educational objectives to Africa:

> Education should be adapted to the mentality, aptitudes, occupations and traditions of the various peoples, conserving as far as possible all sound and healthy elements in the fabric of their social life; adapting them when necessary to changed circumstances and progressive ideas, as an agent of natural growth and evolution. Its aim should be to render the individual more efficient in his or her condition of life, whatever it may be and to promote the advancement of the community as a whole through the improvement of agriculture, the development of native industries, the improvement of health, the training of the people in the management of their own affairs, and the inculcation of true ideals of citizenship and service.[3]

Through religious teaching and moral instruction that are related to his condition of life and daily experience, the African need not be injured in his contact with civilization. Education can strengthen, not weaken, his responsibility to the

---

[3] Advisory Committee on Native Education in the British Tropical African Dependencies, *Education Policy in British Tropical Africa* (London: His Majesty's Stationery Office, 1925), p. 3.

tribal community and his loyalty to the old beliefs; it can also develop the capacity to judge between reality and superstition. Through the discipline of classroom work and through games and recreation he will develop those habits of industry, truthfulness, manliness, and disciplined cooperation which are the foundation of character. The most effective means of achieving these ends, particularly for those who are to be trained for leadership is not, however, the home and village, but the residential school where the example and influence of teachers and the leadership of older pupils create a social life and a tradition in which "standards of judgment are formed and right attitudes acquired almost unconsciously through imbibing the spirit and atmosphere of the school."

The great majority of Africans will of course be educated in village schools taught by native teachers in one of the vernacular languages. English texts may not be appropriate, and the content and method of teaching in all subjects, notably history and geography, will be adapted to the conditions of Africa. The improvement of existing village schools and the development of an efficient system of education can be accomplished only through the cooperation of government and mission. A system of government grants-in-aid will be devised for mission schools that conform to prescribed regulations. To ensure the vitality and efficiency of schools the government will appoint its own inspectorate, but each mission will be expected to develop its own system of supervision. To the extent that conditions in each colony will allow (a significant proviso), a system of education should be developed that would include elementary and secondary education, technical and vocational schools, and higher education, some of which should reach university rank.

It was an ambitious plan with a twofold purpose. While the first task of education is "to raise the standard alike of character and efficiency of the bulk of the people," it must also include "the raising up of capable, trustworthy, public-spirited leaders of the people, belonging to their own race." The objective was to develop a responsible élite through a literary education in residential schools, and at the same time raise the level of the mass through a more practical education related to life on the land. As events were to prove, it became impossible to keep these two goals in balance. Africans grew to resent any kind of schooling different from the European model, and felt that "adaptation" was a plot to give them an inferior education. Kenya's Director of Education at the time confirmed their fears and revealed that when colonial policy was interpreted in Nairobi, it had only limited resemblence to statements enunciated in London:

> The policy of the department in dealing with savage races is rather to educate the masses on practical lines so as to improve their physique, their food supply and their standard of living rather than to hurry the civilization of a select few who become detribalized and divorced from their people. . . . Like children, the untutored savage requires guidance, sympathy, patience, and if he finds that education means a better and more regular food supply, better housing, congenial work and good pay or good crops, the danger of agitation from "mis-fits" is likely to decrease.[4]

And in its *Annual Report* for 1926 the Education Department revealed the methods under which African children should be taught:

> Generally speaking, the African mind in Kenya has reached the stage of sense perception. The imagination and the emotions are both highly developed but the development of the reasoning faculties must be slow. Just as handwork has been found useful in the training of mentally defective children, so the most useful training which the African can receive in his present condition is contact with material processes. . . . Increasing emphasis is being placed in education in Kenya on contact with material processes such as agriculture, handicrafts, sanitation, housework . . . and the classroom will become more and more a place where the ideas and thoughts arising from practical experience can be coordinated and re-

---

[4] *Education Department Annual Report* (Nairobi: Government Printer, 1924).

applied. . . . The training of the African mind, therefore, in its present stage of development is more dependent upon the practical than the literary arts.

It was through the missions that a more liberal view of African education was to come, and perhaps the most significant aspect of the 1925 memorandum was the beginning of a new partnership between the colonial government and the missionary societies through which larger government grants would increase the number and raise the standard of mission schools. In the mid-twenties the government had established two industrial training schools one of which had developed twelve village schools in its area. All other African education was left to the eleven Protestant and four Roman Catholic missions. The oldest of these, the Church Missionary Society, had seventy Europeans working in fifteen mission stations located on the coast, in the highlands, and in the vicinity of Lake Victoria. Related to each station was a central school and satellite village schools, staffed by untrained African teachers, taught in the vernacular, poorly financed, and given only sporadic supervision by the missionary staff. The total enrollment of African children in CMS mission station and village schools in 1925 was some 17,500. The total Government expenditure that year for African education, including a grant to the missions, was £36,000. The African population at this time stood at approximately two million. Europeans and Indians were educated in their own schools and government expenditure for the education of the children of some 10,000 Europeans and 36,000 Asians was, respectively, £24,000 and £11,675. In all, the colonial government was spending only 4 per cent of its revenue on education.

One of the results of the new policy of more liberal grants to the missions was the founding of the first African secondary school. The Church Missionary Society, the Church of Scotland Mission, the Methodist Church Mission Society, and other church bodies joined together to found Alliance High School on land formerly owned by the Kikuyu, 15 miles west of

Nairobi. From its beginning the school served both a Christian and a national purpose and on its Board of Governors sat representatives of Government and the mission societies. Alliance opened on March 1, 1926, with an enrollment of twenty-six boys and a staff of three, all graduates recruited from Britain. The chief subjects of the first two years were to be English and arithmetic, with work also in science, agriculture, and art. In case this appeared too bookish for an African school, the Headmaster explained in his first annual report that Christianity and games were not only a part of the life of a school but were indeed its most important elements. The final two years would be given over to vocational training in the fields of teaching, medicine, agriculture, and forestry. The aim of the school was to produce men of strong Christian character and of wide knowledge and initiative who would become leaders in the African community. By 1940 it had abandoned its vocational training and its boys were writing Cambridge School Certificate examinations. The staff of Alliance knew that if African boys were to rise to leadership in the colony and meet the standards of critical Europeans, they needed the kind of education the European community regarded as the best; that of the British public school. And to this day, as we shall see below, Alliance has been regarded as a model of African education by both the European and African communities.

### Attack on a Vicious Circle

OVER the next twenty years the rural-practical bias recommended in 1925 gave way to the literary-humanistic-religious emphasis of the British tradition in education. When the Beecher Committee made its inquiry into the scope, content, and methods of African education in 1949, it found an almost complete disappearance of a technical emphasis and practical training in primary schools.[5] In the thirties opportunities for

---

[5] *African Education in Kenya,* "The Beecher Report" (Nairobi: Government Printer, 1949).

literate young Africans had begun to open up in the lower reaches of the Civil Service and jobs and training programs became available in the railways and post office, in several government departments and commercial houses, and, of course, in teaching. To qualify for one of these openings an African boy needed to pass the Common Entrance Examination after five years of primary education or, more likely, the Kenya Preliminary Examination (KPE) after a six-year course and two years in a junior secondary school. He could then take a two-year course in teacher training and become a T3 teacher with a beginning salary of £66 per annum. Or if his record on the KPE was exceptionally good he might find a place at Alliance or Mangu and become one of the lucky few (there were thirty-eight in 1948) to pass the School Certificate Examination. And from there he might go on for further training at Makerere College in Uganda. Thus the entry to white-collar employment and further technical and professional training was determined by competitive examinations which were based on a literary curriculum.

It was a system that undermined the practical-rural emphasis of an earlier day—and one that appealed far more to Africans than did a policy of adaptation. As young Africans saw their missionary teachers living in comfortable bungalows furnished in European fashion, or Government officials even more comfortably housed and driving motor cars, their appetite grew for an education that might lead them to a similar way of life. Even a clerkship at, say, £50 a year was infinitely better both in income and prestige than the backbreaking work of subsistence farming:

> While at first the European system of values and schooling was often violently rejected or neglected, a time came when Africans suddenly saw in it their salvation, both from their poverty and from their 'inferiority' to the developed nations. They contrasted, however inarticulately, a world of illiterate, custom-bound subsistence agriculture in the village with a world of towns, clerks, salaries, machines—the 'modern' world. Agriculture came to stand for backwardness and 'bush'; progress started with book-learning in the schools; and the young

teachers and clerks with their better clothes and money salaries (however small) and their scraps of knowledge of a wider world confirmed this view. Nothing could have stopped Africans from seeking the towns and white-collar work; nothing could have stopped the British workman early in this century from trying to get his child education and a white-collar job out of the ruck, out of the dead-end labor of factory or mine. Indeed, just as some of the British workmen, who were the 'Africans' of Britain's nineteenth century, went to Working Men's Colleges . . . so the aspiring African wanted knowledge of the white man's world, and of the sources of his power and of political philosophies which could be used to gain a share of it; he did not want lectures on soil erosion or on manuring his *shamba*.[6]

Those aspirations grew stronger after World War II. Africans who served abroad came in touch with other cultures and saw a technology made possible by a European brand of education. And in the postwar years Kenya was prosperous and more Africans could pay school fees for their children. The result, as the Beecher Committee found, was "a very great demand for education," indeed a desire for universal literacy through a much expanded primary school system. Through a partnership of Government and the voluntary societies, the number of African children in maintained and aided primary schools had grown from 23,164 in 1924 to 150,000 in 1948. But so keen was the African appetite for primary education that a system of unaided primary schools had grown up supported by school fees and local native councils. More than 100,000 children were attending these schools. This rapid expansion of primary education led to a deterioration of standards and the Beecher Committee found that only one-fifth of all primary teachers had themselves attended a full primary course. Inspection was inadequate and the missions were able to employ only eight European grant-aided supervisors. Many mission schools were "grossly overcrowded" and understaffed, double shifts were common in the lower grades, and few schools had

---

[6] Guy Hunter, *Education for a Developing Region, A Study of East Africa* (London: Allen and Unwin, 1963), p. 7.

an adequate supply of books and equipment. All witnesses who appeared before the Beecher Committee spoke of the need to improve the quality of existing schools, rather than to increase their number. The enrollment in primary and secondary schools in 1948, together with the point of examination, is shown below.

TABLE I

*African Primary and Secondary School Enrollment in 1948*

Primary school
    Standard I    113,897
    " II    51,160
    " III    36,849
    " IV    26,018
    " V    21,578   Common Entrance Examination
    " VI    6,983

Junior secondary school
    Form I    3,046
    " II    2,204   Kenya African Preliminary Examination

Senior secondary school
    Form 3    278
    " 4    194   Kenya African Secondary Examination
    " 5    57
    " 6    39   School Certificate Examination

The fall-off in attendance between Standards I and II and after Standard V and Form II is noticeable. It is a pyramid with a small apex, and in a thundering understatement the Committee remarked that "the total number of valuable products of the educational system is very small." The shape of the pyramid created, to change the metaphor, a tightly closed and vicious circle. Local enthusiasm had caused an unofficial expansion of primary education with a great increase in the number of untrained teachers. Because of bad teaching few children were able to qualify for entry to upper primary or secondary schools and it was impossible to increase rapidly the number of qualified teachers:

The bottom of the system cannot be improved until the top has been enlarged; the top cannot be enlarged until the bottom has been improved. The Committee sees its task, therefore, to be the selection of a point at which to break this circle and to recommend how it should be done.[7]

The Committee attacked the circle at not one but several points. To improve the quality of primary education it recommended that the duties of inspection and management be made more efficient through the employment of more European and African staff. Inspection should be the function of the Education Department; management and supervision could be left to the voluntary agencies. Teacher training must be improved and the lowest grade of qualified teacher, the T4, must have at least eight years of primary education followed by two years of training. The school system should be reorganized into primary, intermediate, and secondary divisions, each of four years. At the end of each stage, effective selection should take place to ensure that those qualified pass on to the next higher stage. In making estimates of the proportion of African children who could benefit from a secondary education the Committee broke new ground. It cited the work of Cyril Burt on the distribution of educational abilities and came to the conclusion that the distribution of ability among African children did not differ markedly from that of the child population of a London borough.[8] Regardless of absolute standards of attainment, the same proportion of children in each culture could profit from education beyond the primary school. Although it interpreted Burt's research rather arbitrarily and proposed that only the upper quartile of those who completed the four-year primary course should enter the intermediate school, and again the upper quartile of Standard VIII leavers should qualify for the secondary school, the Committee's recommendations would lead to a twelvefold increase in sec-

---

[7] *African Education in Kenya, op. cit.*, p. 12.

[8] Cyril Burt, *The Distribution and Relations of Educational Abilities* (London: London County Council, 1917).

ondary school enrollment within ten years. It was a different outlook from the "savage races" view of an earlier period.

The Beecher Committee found no fault with the alliance between Government and the missionary societies and reaffirmed the objectives of the White Paper of 1925 in stressing the importance of religious teaching and moral instruction. The administration of primary and intermediate education should become the responsibility of district education boards on which the missionary societies and African district councils would have equal representation. Costs should be met from pupils' fees and grants from central and local governments. Government aid should flow to schools previously unaided, primary education must be made more efficient, and the number of secondary schools should grow. It would all be possible if the colony were prepared to double its expenditure on African education within a decade.

### The Tempo Quickens

IN the five years before Independence new doors opened to an ever-increasing number of Africans in central and local government, in agriculture, in the public service organizations, and in the larger commercial firms. The wounds of the Mau Mau emergency were healing, and there was talk and hope of a multiracial society. There was also very considerable pressure from the African nationalist movement for greater educational opportunity. As self-government and independence came in sight, the pace of educational change quickened in order to produce the secondary school leavers and university graduates who would Africanize the Civil Service and fill the manpower quotas which economists were busily devising. It was easy to recruit primary school leavers but a higher qualification than KPE now was needed. If expatriates were to be replaced in the public service, and if Africans were to be trained for the professions and occupations that were now open to them, educational goals had to be related to manpower demands. Secondary school output became crucially important for it was those with a secondary education who could go on to become university graduates or enter training for a widening range of technical, business, or administrative careers.

The expansion of secondary schools and the marked increase, in fact a trebling, of the number of School Certificate passes can be seen in Table II. Higher School Certificate classes began in 1961 in five African schools.

TABLE II [9]

*Development of African Secondary Education 1958–1963*

|  | Number of Aided Secondary Schools | Form I Enrollment | School Certificate Passes | Higher School Certificate Candidates |
|---|---|---|---|---|
| 1958 | 22 | 1,291 | 491 |  |
| 1959 | 27 | 1,726 | 654 |  |
| 1960 | 32 | 1,712 | 649 |  |
| 1961 | 50 | 2,194 | 951 |  |
| 1962 | 68 | 3,415 | 1,072 | 141 |
| 1963 | 81 | 3,510 | 1,528 | 199 |

[9] The figures throughout this section, and there are many, are derived from the Annual Summaries and Triennial Surveys of the Education Department as it was known in 1960 and the Ministry of Education thereafter. See also Guy Hunter, *op. cit.*

The number of students enrolled in higher education increased almost fourfold over the five-year period, largely through a phenomenal increase in bursary and scholarship awards for study overseas. Through airlifts of students organized by Tom Mboya, then Secretary of the Kenya African National Union (KANU), the number of Kenya students in the United States rose from sixty in 1956 to over 1,000 in 1963. This overseas rush probably accounted for a temporary decline in enrollments at Makerere and the Royal Technical College, Nairobi. The University of East Africa was formally opened in 1963 with three constituent colleges: Makerere University College, Uganda; University College, Nairobi (formerly Royal Technical College); and University College, Dar es Salaam, Tanzania.

TABLE III
*Africans in Higher Education 1958–1963*

|  | Makerere | Royal Technical College | United Kingdom | Other Countries | Total |
|---|---|---|---|---|---|
| 1958–1959 | 294 | 50 | 74 | 145 | 563 |
| 1959–1960 | 324 | 72 | 94 | 252 | 742 |
| 1960–1961 | 368 | 96 | 126 | 640 | 1,230 |
| 1961–1962 | 280 | 122 | 220 | 1,356 | 1,978 |
| 1962–1963 | 189 | 115 | 369 | 1,454 | 2,127 |

As secondary and higher education expanded there were changes of a different kind in the primary schools. The Beecher Committee's proposal to change the structure to a primary, intermediate, and secondary system had been adopted, and the shape of the educational pyramid changed. In 1958 only 29 per cent of African children went beyond Standard IV; by 1963 the proportion was 80 per cent, and plans were well in hand for introducing a new combined primary/intermediate course of seven years, eliminating the examination at the end of Standard IV and thus allowing all children entering Standard I to complete a full primary education. The over-all increase in primary and intermediate school enrolment during the five-year period was, however, less than 25 per cent, and *fewer* children entered Standard I in 1963 than in 1958—probably because of an increase in school fees. The inspection and supervision of primary schools had, as recommended by Beecher, been improved, and there was a marginal improvement in the quality of teaching—if teacher qualifications are an index of classroom performance. In 1962, the proportion of primary teachers who were untrained primary school leavers stood at 40 per cent. There was, however, a decided decrease in unaided schools and by 1963 practically all

African primary and intermediate schools were managed by district education boards or the voluntary agencies and financed by pupils' fees, subventions from African district councils and the central Government. Costs had far exceeded the Beecher predictions. In 1960 the total expenditure on African education by the central and local Governments was about 4 million, approximately four times the figure proposed by the Committee in its ten-year development plan.

It was during this period that a radical change was introduced in the content and method of lower primary education. English as the language of instruction began to replace the vernacular in Standard I and a movement known first as English Medium and later as the New Primary Approach brought not only a new language policy but "activity methods" and a new, more liberal and lively spirit to primary school classrooms. With materials prepared by the Special Centre of the Inspectorate the movement quickly won the support of parents, teachers, and children and, as Chapter Three reveals, it has attracted attention from several parts of the world.

By 1963 all technical education was at the postprimary level and some 900 boys with a KPE pass were enrolled in seven trade schools preparing for artisan employment in industry or self-employment in a trade or craft. The majority of these boys entered the building trades. There were four academic secondary schools with a technical bias offering technical subjects up to School Certificate level, but the most comprehensive centre for technical training was the Kenya Polytechnic which opened in 1961, and by 1963 had nearly a thousand students studying engineering, domestic science, and commercial subjects at a nondegree level.

Until 1960 education in Kenya was administered and financed on racial lines. For European children between the ages of seven and fifteen education was compulsory. Practically all pupils who completed the seven-year primary course were admitted to a European secondary school in Kenya or a public school in Britain. The secondary schools in Kenya offered both grammar and modern streams, the former leading to School Certificate and the latter emphasizing industrial arts for boys and commercial and homecraft courses for girls. Perhaps a quarter of the grammar stream boys went into the sixth form and from there to university in Britain. The residential secondary schools tended to be very similar in atmosphere and emphasis to the British public schools and in establishing such schools as the Kenya High School (1930), the Prince of Wales (1931), and the Duke of York (1949), the European community revealed its determination to educate its sons and daughters not only in British fashion but on a standard fully comparable with the schools of the United Kingdom. As we shall see in a later chapter, these schools with their spacious grounds, sturdy buildings, and comfortable staff houses were a ringing testimony to the Europeans' belief that they had come to Kenya to stay. The high-water mark of enrollment came in 1960 when 13,000 European children attended thirty-eight primary and fourteen secondary schools. Thereafter, with Independence in the wind and the future uncertain, European families began to leave Kenya and by 1963 attendance in these schools had fallen to 9,900. Now, of course, they are fully integrated and in official circles are referred to as the former European schools.

It was in Asian primary schools in Nairobi that the first experiments were undertaken in using English as the medium of instruction from the first day a child entered school in Standard I. As the movement gathered momentum it spread to all Asian schools throughout Kenya and, with different texts and teachers' manuals, was adapted to African schools. Education was compulsory for Asian boys between seven and fifteen in Nairobi, Kisumu, and Mombasa until 1963, and almost as many girls as boys were enrolled. Secondary schools, most of which were day and not residential, offered grammar and modern streams. Buildings and equipment were rather less lavish than at European schools. In comparison with African secondary school students who were the top 10 per cent of a large group of primary school leavers, and with European students who were being schooled in their own language, Asian students did not fare so well on the School Certificate examinations.

The system of administering education on racial lines began to change in 1960 when the European and African sections in the Ministry of Education disappeared and assistant directors were appointed for all primary, secondary, and technical schools. Two years later the Asian section was dissolved. It was in 1961 that a start was made in the training and appointment of Africans to administrative positions in the Ministry. Asian and African students were first admitted to European secondary schools in 1960, and to European primary schools in 1962.

Africans and Europeans have judged Britain's trusteeship by very different criteria. Europeans point to the dedication of missionaries and their introduction of an education that was grounded in moral and spiritual values, to the creation of a school system that in 1963 enrolled more than three quarters of a million young people, and to the development of an African leadership trained sufficiently to become the new rulers. European education brought to the colonies the humanistic tradition of the West with its stress on human dignity and freedom. As Africans embraced this tradition, they rejected, as had Europeans before them, whatever circumstances hold the human spirit in bondage—whether these are miserable social and economic conditions or political subjugation. Thus in British colonies where Western values have been transmitted through a humanistic education, inevitably there has developed a demand for freedom and independence. And the demand has included not only freedom from political subservience but an improvement in living standards and a release from ignorance, hunger, and disease.[10]

---

[10] For a more extended statement of this view, see P. C. C. Evans, "Western Education and Rural Productivity in Tropical Africa," *Africa*, XXXII (October, 1962), pp. 313–323.

The new African leadership would reply that devoted as they were, the missionaries nevertheless condoned the segregationist policies of the colonial regime and did little to build within Africans a sense of pride and confidence in their own culture. Too often they regarded African custom and tradition as primitive and uncivilized. Although the humanistic tradition of the West may enshrine values of human dignity, Kenya officials and settlers did not live by those values when they established a segregated society that stratified education and social life on racial lines. In the ten years before Independence more capital was invested in European and Asian education, representing 3 per cent of the population, than in education of the African 97 per cent. Admittedly, the partnership of Government and missions allowed a larger number of African children to attend primary school than was the case in many of the colonies, but in the year Kenya won her independence only 12 per cent of primary school leavers could enter secondary school. To the African, these were strange ways of upholding the paramountcy of his interests and of maintaining the principle of trusteeship as enunciated in 1923.

# PART TWO. PRIMARY EDUCATION

[CHAPTER TWO]

## Primary Schools: Teachers and Children

At Independence some 50 per cent of the children in the primary school age group were attending school, and there were strong pressures to increase that proportion, in fact to move as rapidly as possible towards universal primary education. The Kenya African National Union Manifesto of 1963 stated unequivocally, "KANU intends that every child in Kenya shall have a minimum of seven years' free education." Fortunately no dateline was added. The case for primary education for all children was stated by the Ominde Commission:

> Looking out over the next thirty or forty years we see a radical transformation of our national life, for which large numbers of our citizens will remain permanently unfitted, unless provided in their maturity with opportunities for training. Save in rare, exceptional instances, the minimum foundation for such training consists of the fundamental education in respect to literacy, numeracy, manual dexterity and general knowledge of the world furnished by the primary school. Thus to use an economic metaphor, a primary education is the minimum basic educational requirement for take-off into the modern sector of our national life. Those that lack such advantages are liable to remain for the rest of their days largely outside the range of modern ways of living, unable to benefit from training or to share greatly in the rewards of a developed economy and becoming in the end an impoverished residue of a bygone age.[1]

But if the "take-off" is to be successful the quality of primary education must be maintained at a reasonable level, and

---

[1] *Kenya Education Commission Report, Part II* (Nairobi: Government Printer, 1965), para. 539.

in the years immediately following Independence as primary schools expanded and experienced teachers left the profession, there was a deep concern over a deterioration of standards. Until the final years of the colonial period teaching was one of the comparatively few professions open to Africans and primary schools frequently were staffed, particularly at the upper level, with well-qualified men. With Independence, as we have seen, many new jobs particularly in government service became available and schools lost the cream of their staff. In 1964, 75 per cent of the members of the National Assembly were former teachers. For the secondary school leaver with a first or second division School Certificate in his hand, the prospect of two years of training followed by a teaching job in a rural school had little appeal. There were other ways he could help in nation building, and besides, life in the towns was more attractive. By 1965 only 8 per cent of the primary teachers had completed secondary school. Perhaps even more serious was the proportion (34 per cent) of teachers without training of any kind. This meant that the average primary school staff had seven teachers qualified as follows (the KT1, T2, T3, and T4 qualifications changed to P1, etc. in 1964):

| | |
|---|---|
| P1 (School Certificate and two years of training) | |
| P2 (two or three years of secondary school and two years of training) | 2 |
| P3 (complete primary school and two years of training) | |
| P4 (incomplete primary school and two years of training) | 3 |
| Unqualified (primary school but no training) | 2 |

The P3 teachers were usually placed in the lower primary grades, the P1 or P2 teachers taught Standards VI and VII, and unqualified teachers were assigned to Standards IV and V, frequently with disastrous results. It was in IV and V that the changeover took place from vernacular to English as the medium of instruction, and the unqualified teacher, who was usually a primary school leaver getting a year or two of teaching experience before he was old enough to enroll in a training college, was out of his depth.

Although teachers' houses were provided, they had fallen all too often into what the Ominde Commission described as "a shocking state of disrepair." Salaries were low in spite of a new scale which had been introduced in 1964.

| Qualification | Salary Scale |
|---|---|
| P1 | £348–£726 |
| P2 | £240–£456 |
| P3 | £162–£264 |
| P4 | £120–£180 |
| Unqualified | £84 |

It is not surprising therefore that the Commission was concerned over primary school teachers' morale:

> Let us consider for a moment what we are asking of this profession. We are asking them, with often insufficient basic education and often no training at all, to take on a responsible and difficult duty—the educating of our children. To that end, we put them often in grossly inadequate classrooms, with unsuitable and sometimes insufficient furnishings, and we ask them to teach, frequently without enough textbooks, or with none at all, and supply only the minimum of teaching materials. Finally, all too often we expect them to live in inadequate and unsuitable houses. We do not wish to invite self pity, but these are the facts as we found them. . . .
>
> *Nothing is more important than putting new heart into our primary teachers* and few changes can make a greater difference to the schools. We therefore urge attention . . . not only to improve the physical context of primary education but also, and especially, to raise the spirits of the men and women, to whom we have entrusted the education of our children.[2]

Over the next several years a variety of measures were undertaken in an attempt to raise the morale and the competence of primary teachers. The Salary Review Commission in a

---

[2] *Ibid.*, Part I, para. 151–152.

report submitted in August, 1967, recommended salary increases for teachers totalling £778,000 in an attempt to make the teaching profession "as attractive as any other career in the public service." The Government of Kenya accepted the Commission's proposals and the P3 scale was increased by £18 in the first year, £21 in the second, and £24 in each of the subsequent nine years.

There has been a marked improvement in the qualifications of candidates entering the training colleges. P4 candidates are no longer admitted and the quality of P3 and P2 classes has improved. At Kagumo College, for example, 1,500 applicants applied for the fifty P3 places in 1967, and only those students who passed the new Kenya Junior Secondary Examination at the end of Form II were admitted to P2 places. In 1964, some 40 per cent of the P1 students at Kagumo had failed School Certificate, but in 1967 the proportion was only 2 per cent.

Kenya has decided that the function of the primary school is to give "a fundamental education in respect of literacy, numeracy, manual dexterity and general knowledge of the world." This kind of education, it is believed, will serve both that small minority who will find a place in a secondary school and the 85 or 90 per cent whose formal education will stop at Standard VII. There is no place in the curriculum for technical or vocational training, and agriculture, which was formerly taught as a separate subject, is now one of the topics dealt with under general science. Both geography and history are more "African" in content than previously, and a new and experimental syllabus has been introduced in mathematics.

The major emphasis is given to English, mathematics, and science and the 1967 syllabus notes that "the day should start with the most mentally demanding work." For the extensive reading periods in English in the afternoon, the Language Section of the Curriculum Development and Research Centre in Nairobi has devised a system of book boxes suitable for class libraries. These are selected from a list of 300 graded books,

## Primary Schools: Teachers and Children / 29

more than half of which have African settings. In order to emphasize the change from colonial days, the compiler of this list explains that the books have settings in many different parts of the world, "not just England." The Mathematics Section is developing a new primary course emphasizing "discovery methods which enable children to reason out mathematical ideas and processes and make the computative skills more meaningful." In 1966 the experimental materials, which stemmed originally from a conference held by Educational Services Incorporated but have since been revised, were in use in twenty-five schools. The aims set forth for science teaching are equally innovative—and, hopefully, reassuring to the P3 or P2 teacher:

> The subject matter of science is the world that man lives in and his attempt to understand and control it. This study has its proper methods and its own attitude of mind. The teacher's outlook matters more than the amount of his knowledge; his hope is to train children to see with their own eyes, find things out for themselves, and report what they have observed rather than what they have been told . . . put the children into situations where they can observe. Another is to try to demonstrate the principles underlying what the children see. A third is to help the children to record what they have seen, and to begin to draw conclusions from it. . . .
>
> The modern world cannot be understood without some understanding of science. The spirit of inquiry needs to be encouraged as early as possible. Accurate observations, backed by clear thinking, help to sweep away superstition and open the door to true knowledge of the world we live in.[3]

The study of geography begins in Standard III with the area immediately surrounding the school, moves out to other parts of Kenya, and then in Standard IV, to other parts of Africa. Standard V gives an introduction to the "New Lands": America, Australia, and New Zealand; and Standard VI to the "Old Lands" of Asia and Europe. Pupils return in Standard VII

---

[3] *Syllabus for Kenya Primary Schools* (Nairobi: Ministry of Education, 1967), pp. 111–112.

for a more detailed study of Africa and East Africa in particular. The emphasis is on pupil activity and projects which in Standard III include visits, model making, drawing, painting, dramatic work, and writing—all in connection with, say, an airport and a game park.

In history, teachers are admonished not to dictate notes but rather to encourage imaginative work by the children. This will include written work, drawings, maps, diagrams, and time charts. For the study, in Standard III, of the traditional ways of life of the major tribal groups of Kenya, ten tribal histories are listed for use by teachers, four of which are written by Africans. Standard IV moves out to the ancient civilizations of Egypt, Mesopotamia, Greece, and Rome. Standard V returns to Africa—the explorers, traders, and missionaries, and Standards VI and VII concentrate on East Africa in the nineteenth and twentieth centuries. No modern history of Europe or America is included.

Under the Education Act of 1968 the management of primary schools was entrusted to local authorities, that is, county and municipal councils. These authorities, acting on behalf of the Teachers Service Commission, pay teachers' salaries and are responsible for the provision of equipment, the supervision of schools, and the opening of new schools, all of which were formerly the responsibility of churches. If it is the wish of parents that the religious tradition of the school be continued, the local authority may appoint a church to serve as the sponsor of the school. The sponsor is consulted on matters of staffing and is able to use school premises in out-of-school hours. Religious education is provided in a school that has a sponsor. Thus, in transferring the management of primary schools from missions to local authorities, the act does not, necessarily, remove the teaching of religion from the schools. Religious education is regarded as a regular subject in both the upper and lower primary grades and three periods are allocated to it each week. Detailed syllabuses are provided for Protestant and Catholic schools, and other religious communities may develop their own syllabus and submit it to the Minister for approval. Discussions have begun between Protestant and Roman Catholic leaders with a view to developing a "unified syllabus" which, it is hoped, will be sanctioned in all schools sponsored by Christian churches.

At the end of primary school all children write the same Kenya Preliminary Examination, preliminary, that is, to secondary education for those who can secure places. At the moment some 10 to 15 per cent of primary leavers find places in aided secondary schools, and thus in its importance in deciding a child's future the KPE is little short of the Final Reckoning. A paper in English, another in mathematics, and a general paper which includes history, geography, and science are written one day in mid-November. All papers have now abandoned essay questions and have become fully objective, partly as a means of discouraging cramming through the memorization of model answers, and partly because it became impossible to mark over 300,000 papers, tabulate the results, and use them in deciding secondary school selection for the term beginning in January. Within a year or two the KPE will probably be machine scored. Sample questions from recent papers are given below:

### Mathematics

What is the next number in the following series?
1, 2, 3, 5, 8, 13, ...

15 ( )
16 ( )
19 ( )
21 ( )

Which of the answers given do you consider to be the nearest to the correct answer to the problem?

$$\frac{4\frac{1}{5} \times 6\frac{12}{13}}{1\frac{9}{10}}$$

12 ( )
14 ( )
24 ( )
28 ( )

### History

The main purpose of Joseph Thompson's
journey of 1883–1884 was to
- discover the source of the Nile ( )
- find a direct route from the Coast to Lake Victoria ( )
- make friends with the Masai ( )
- reach the shores of Lake Baringo ( )

### Geography

Mombasa has a higher temperature than
Nairobi because Mombasa is
- nearer the sea ( )
- further south ( )
- lower in altitude ( )
- more humid ( )

### Science

The valve of a bicycle inner tube keeps the
air in the tube because of
- high pressure inside the tube ( )
- atmospheric pressure ( )
- a metal screw ( )
- balance between pressures ( )

The KPE is both a means of upholding the academic standards of primary schools, and a device for certifying that children have satisfactorily completed a primary education. Every candidate who sits the examination is awarded a Certificate of Primary Education which records his grades on the three examination papers. The examination is also an instrument, although a blunt one, for deciding secondary school selection. The dual function of KPE is a reflection of the ambivalence of the primary schools. They are attempting to provide, as a Preface to the Syllabus states, "a balanced primary school course for the child's full development," knowing that most children will finish their formal education in Standard VII, and at the same time offer bright children "an adequate preparation for the next stage of education."

When a visitor enters a rural primary school classroom he is immediately struck with what these children and their teachers do not have. The youngsters are dressed in the simplest of uniforms: boys in khaki shirts and shorts, frequently tattered, girls in faded pink or blue jumpers. In country districts school children rarely wear shoes. Three or four classrooms are joined in one unit and are bare in their simplicity. The walls are either of mud plastered over wattle, or rough slabs of timber placed upright. The tin roof, often pitted with holes, has a generous overhang and serves as a sun breaker. A classroom may have a door but seldom windows; instead, openings about the size of windows are cut in the wall to let in light, but the result is a dimly lit room.

There is little equipment other than what the teacher and class make, rarely a teacher's desk, no ceiling to hide the tin roof, no floor except hard-packed earth, and, of course, no electric light. There are only the essentials: desks, blackboards, a cupboard for books, and a teacher. The desks are narrow tables with even narrower benches attached, and blackboards are seldom more than 4 feet square, but the books are good. A score of commercial publishing houses now operating in East Africa have produced texts, many of them by African authors. These are well written and illustrated and are quite satisfactory tools for primary education: the trouble is that schools seldom have enough of them. The maximum that local authorities can spend on books is 15/ per pupil per year, and many authorities spend less.

Classes of forty or more are not uncommon but African children are well-behaved, eager to answer, and usually stand up and deliver their answers in complete sentences. They are both less restless and less critical than the precocious young sceptics of Britain or America. They give the impression of being glad to be at school, grateful that their fathers can pay the 60/ yearly fee, and anxious to learn whatever their elders tell them to learn because education and examinations are keys that will unlock the way to a better life.

In 1967 primary school enrollment reached 1,133,179, an increase of more than 200,000 since 1963. Nevertheless, Kenya was schooling less than 60 per cent of her children aged seven to thirteen. Universal primary education still remains a long-term objective.

[CHAPTER THREE]

## The New Primary Approach

> Nobody, who is familiar with the primary school, will be unaware of the occurrence of drill methods of teaching; of an authoritarian tone of voice on the part of the teacher; of a neglect of activity methods and pupil participation; of little attempt at grouping or otherwise adjusting instruction to the needs of particular children; of a negative approach to discipline; and of a formalized presentation of material.[1]

THE typical primary school teacher in a developing country was, and frequently still is, poorly educated and low paid. His education was confined to a primary school and a period of training, and he tends to teach as he was taught in a dull and formal fashion. He is satisfied if his pupils acquire mechanical skills in reading, writing, and arithmetic and memorize a few facts in history and geography. If the Ministry of Education has provided him with a syllabus he clings to it and to one or two official texts. The only questions he is sure of being able to answer are those he asks himself. The teacher is a victim of his own very limited education and, because his own knowledge is so thin, he has neither the intellectual nor the emotional security which will enable him to create a classroom climate of activity, curiosity, and exploration:

> These complaints from emergent countries in all corners of the world that primary education tends to begin and end with rote memorizing are so consistent that one is led to look for some cause common to all the cases, and most educators would

---
[1] *Kenya Education Commission Report, Part I,* para. 180.

probably agree that the bulk of the blame lies with the low level of education and the inadequate professional training of the teachers.[2]

A further cause of formalism in the schools of East Africa goes back to the nature of tribal instruction, much of which was prescriptive; the young sat at the feet of the elders and were "told."

When leaders of a developing country, possibly influenced by their own education and experience abroad, decide that their primary schools are too bound by tradition and need to be reformed, two alternatives are open to them. They can put a brake on the expansion of primary schools and resist the pressures of parents and politicians for universal primary education. For the next several years they accept the present low quality of teaching and put high priority on producing new teachers with a higher level of general education. Only candidates with a secondary school certificate are accepted into the teacher training colleges on the assumption that the way to improve the quality of primary education is to raise the educational level of the teaching profession. Under this strategy a developing country admits that it cannot leap across the century that was necessary for the more developed countries to reform their primary schools.

The alternative is to accept two hard realities: political and social pressures will not allow primary education to stand still while the country waits for teachers to become better educated; and a poor country cannot afford to pay a primary school teaching force made up predominantly of secondary school leavers. Moreover, changes can be brought to primary education through new methods and techniques and, so the argument runs, it is possible to train teachers, who are themselves poorly educated, to use these techniques effectively. Through intensive training practising teachers may, for example, be taught how to teach the "new" mathematics and sci-

---

[2] C. E. Beeby, *The Quality of Education in Developing Countries* (Cambridge, Mass.: Harvard University Press, 1966), p. 85.

ence. Educational Services Incorporated, working cooperatively with African educators, has set up workshops, which are based on the principle of giving highly specific training within a modern or "activity" context:

> Training or retraining of teachers should focus narrowly on the use of the materials they will be using in the classroom, rather than on the broad range of the subject they will be teaching. (More concretely stated, if we prepare materials for use in teaching elementary science, we wish the teachers to be trained in the use of those materials rather than in "science".)
>
> Learning should take place on a no-holds-barred basis. The student should be encouraged to rely on more than his text books—to use his ears, his nose, his hands, his finger-tips, and above all his active, inquiring mind.[3]

Of the two alternatives, Kenya has chosen the second, and has decided that trained primary school leavers will continue to staff the primary schools for some years to come. The long-term goal is, however, the improvement of the general education of its teachers.

## English Medium and Activity Methods

IN the mid-1950's a sense of dissatisfaction began to grow in Kenya over the examination performance of Asian and African children. In these pre-Independence years European, Asian, and African children were taught in three separate and nonintegrated school systems. In European schools English was, of course, the language of instruction and French and Latin were introduced in Standard VI. Asian primary pupils were taught in one of four vernaculars—Gujarati, Punjabi, Hindi, Urdu—and English was taught as a subject for two or three years, and then became the medium of instruction. In African schools the children were taught initially in one of some twenty tribal lan-

---

[3] *Quarterly Report of Educational Services Incorporated* (Cambridge, Mass., 1964), p. 109.

guages, or in Swahili. English which was at first a separate subject became the language of instruction in the fifth year and the African vernacular continued to be taught as a second language. In the examinations at the end of the primary school, Asian and African pupils revealed marked weaknesses in the use of English. Again at the end of secondary school similar weaknesses showed up and over 75 per cent of those who failed to win a Cambridge School Certificate did so because of a failure on the compulsory English language paper. Few students had either the confidence or the ability to attempt the oral English examination and, of those who did, more than half failed. Something, apparently, was wrong with the teaching of English, and in 1957 the Ministry of Education created a Special Centre as an offshoot of the inspectorate to investigate and experiment. The Centre staff focused their attention first on Asian primary schools and discovered that pupils had little oral training in English and instead were memorizing items of information in a written language they did not understand. The very considerable linguistic problem involved in requiring a child to change from one language of instruction to another halfway through the primary school had been overlooked:

> The process of changing from one medium of learning to another has usually resulted in the loss of about one year, measured purely in terms of time. But in terms of psychological, linguistic and educational disturbance, this transfer, in amateur hands has been at best a diluted blessing and at worst a disaster.
>
> Perhaps the main damage in the transfer from one teaching medium to another has lain in the loss of meaning. Meaning is understood or learnt by a process of association in which the new language symbol is met in the context of the experience which it symbolizes. Thus the teaching of the second language which is to become the vehicle of all educational thought and expression should involve the presentation of both form and meaning and their subsequent fusion into language habits. When only form is taught, oral and written expression became an abstract exercise dealing tentatively with artificial class-

room values rather than real life situations: indeed intelligent and intelligible expression in the new language are virtually impossible.[4]

This diagnosis of the problem and the evidence from examination performance were sufficient to convince the Director of Education that the Centre should experiment with English medium teaching from the beginning of Standard I. It was a difficult decision because a considerable body of opinion, including that of UNESCO linguistic authorities, supported the view that a child's education should begin in his native language. His adjustment to school is difficult under any circumstances and it will be only more difficult if he is given the formidable task of learning a new language. Furthermore, if on his first day in school he is asked to put aside his mother tongue and adopt another language for learning, he may be driven to feel that there is something inferior about his language and, perhaps, himself.

This orthodoxy did not, however, deter the Special Centre from going forward with the experiment. A grant of £7,190 from the Ford Foundation provided printing equipment, tape recorders, and additional staff. The first step was "to break down and reassemble" English structures within the limits of carefully selected word lists so that a child could be taught to talk in simple terms about the familiar aspects of his immediate environment, and to exchange experience through communication with others. As the staff travelled abroad and studied current practice in the teaching of language and modern methods in primary schools they made a major decision. Why not link the new program in English with modern educational practice, that is, with group teaching through "activity" methods? The first step was to select for training twenty-five teachers from eight Asian schools in Nairobi. These lower primary teachers taught their classes in the mornings, frequently under supervision, and came to the Centre every afternoon to confer

---

[4] Charles O'Hagan, "English Medium Teaching in Kenya," *Overseas Education*, XXXIV (October, 1962), pp. 101–102.

with one another and the staff. Their instruction included speech drills, lessons in English grammar and syntax, the making of teaching aids, and guidance in the teaching of English. Members of the Centre staff found them "tremendously keen" even to the extent of recruiting their friends to collect throw-away materials for making classroom apparatus. During the afternoon sessions they planned their work for the following day. Over a two-year period they were able to test the course books and readers in preparation at the Centre before these were adopted in the schools and introduced into the syllabus of the Asian teacher training college for women in Nairobi. In 1961, four years after the Centre was opened, Oxford University Press announced the *Peak Series,* a group of books designed "to meet the needs of Asian children in East Africa who begin their primary education in English, without prior knowledge of that language." One year later 80 per cent of Asian primary classes in Kenya were following *Peak* and the Asian training colleges had incorporated it into their syllabuses. One student teacher, more puzzled than enthusiastic about the break with tradition, reported to a member of the Centre staff, "I don't like English Medium teaching. It leads to bad discipline; today a child walked up to my table and asked a question."

### Peak *and* New Peak

*Peak* was planned and written by Charles O'Hagan, director of the Special Centre, and his colleagues Daphne Penn and Ralph Malone. When completed in 1963 the series contained twenty-five books for the first three years of the primary school; eleven were for teachers and the others were children's readers. The teachers' books gave detailed instructions on teaching English and other subjects through English. The vocabulary and the sentence patterns for each stage were given, as were classroom techniques and methods for creating natural situations for the use of oral English and ways of making lessons interesting and attractive to lower primary children. The reading books used the vocabulary, structures, and patterns that were taught in the oral language lessons. A picture book was designed to prepare the children of Standard I for reading and a Link Reader introduced them to the printed word. Then followed the first reader with an associated workbook of practice exercises, and a supplementary reader, *I Live in East Africa*. A similar set of readers and duplicated teachers' notes followed for Standards II and III.

*Peak* made a double contribution. It used English as the medium of instruction from the first day of Standard I, but it also introduced a new kind of education into the schools of East Africa. The principles, the methods, and the paraphernalia of progressive education were incorporated into the program; the child should become an active and an equal partner in his own learning; much of his education was to come through the senses; varied occupations and activities should take up the first hour of the school day; and classes were to be divided into small groups as a means of improving instruction and developing qualities of self-reliance and cooperation. A warm and informal class atmosphere would encourage children to express themselves and ask questions. School should, in short, be a place where a child could learn and enjoy himself with a new set of brothers and sisters.

This new kind of education soon became known as the English Medium program or method. The term was misleading, as the Centre staff were at pains to point out. The main emphasis during the lower primary years was not to be placed on the learning of English but on the development and unfolding of the child. The language side, the staff insisted, should be the servant of the educational side, and it was this combination that gave the program its pioneering and "breakthrough" quality.

> Our aim in the Special Centre is not primarily to teach English but to educate through the medium of English. Fluency in English is a by-product of our system, not its chief end. If

children can use a language for all they want to do and say, in an atmosphere where inquiry and activity are encouraged, they will learn the language fast enough. This is what we have tried to do; to link language to all the needs of young children. This is why we think our work is revolutionary. The children work in small groups as individuals, and feel free to express themselves through positive constructive activities. The same English structures recur repeatedly through the day, no matter what the child's timetable is framed to teach.[5]

At no time did the Special Centre feel that the new program should be confined to Asian schools only. The problems of extending it to African schools were, however, formidable. Asian schools were mainly confined to the towns and easily accessible but the African schools were widely scattered and, of course, far more numerous. The major problem lay in the different qualifications of teachers. Most Asian primary teachers had completed four years of secondary school and two years of training, whereas African teachers, in the main, had only a primary education and a two-year course of training. And the Centre staff knew that it would have to adapt both the text and the pictures of *Peak* to the experience of African children. With the help of a second grant of £7,900 from the Ford Foundation the work began in 1961, and in the same year one African Standard I class in Nairobi was turned over to English Medium teaching. Oxford managed to publish a Standard I course book for African schools early in 1962 and eighty classes began using it. This was the beginning of the *New Peak Series* adapted from *Peak* by Arnold Curtis and similar to it in its approach to teaching language and using activity methods. The settings were changed and people and places became African rather than Asian. The instructions to teachers were rewritten with African P3 teachers in mind. By the time all twenty-five titles of *New Peak* were available demand for the course had grown enormously and communities were tempted to adopt it before their teachers were adequately pre-

---

[5] Charles O'Hagan, *op. cit.*, p. 103.

pared. The Centre proposed that three conditions should be met before teachers with only a primary education themselves could manage the techniques and language content of *New Peak:* they should have had a course of professional training; the training, whether preservice or in-service, should include instruction in spoken English and in *New Peak* methods; and teachers must have help and supervision during the first year of their experience with the new course. To meet these conditions, even minimally, would require a national effort in which the Centre, the training colleges, the Ministry of Education and of course the teachers themselves would all need to cooperate.

The Centre organized "conversion" courses for Standard I teachers and supervisors and sent its staff into all sections of the country to demonstrate new primary methods and to teach both the content and the procedures of *New Peak.* The training colleges responded quickly. By 1963, with only one or two exceptions, they had started to revise their syllabuses and to include *New Peak* and its implications as a part of the training of lower primary teachers. Training college tutors went out to the schools to supervise English Medium teachers and their reports began to filter into the Centre. African P3 teachers could stand comparison with Asian P1's. They were using equipment and apparatus well; were finding it difficult, however, to give children individual attention; and were learning how to handle the language lessons. The African oral tradition had given them a good ear.

## Growth and Acceptance

MEANWHILE, Standard I EM classes had increased to 220 in 1963 and would increase eightfold in the next two years. One area of rapid development was Nyeri County in Central Province. Under the stimulus and supervision of Millo Shaw, a Canadian tutor on the staff of Kagumo Training College, the program developed as shown below. By 1966, 95 per cent of all Standard I's were EM classes.

### English Medium Classes in Nyeri County

|  |  | 1962 | 1963 | 1964 | 1965 | 1966 |
|---|---|---|---|---|---|---|
| Standard | I | 4 | 45 | 150 | 309 | 319 |
| Standard | II |  | 4 | 45 | 150 | 309 |
| Standard | III |  |  | 4 | 45 | 150 |
| Standard | IV |  |  |  | 4 | 45 |
| Standard | V |  |  |  |  | 4 |

This growth reflects a very considerable popular demand for the new program. The primary schools of Nyeri are under the management of a county council, and unless the council has evidence of support from parents it will not instruct its education officer to start a course which uses English as the teaching language. Parents in Nyeri have made it clear that they want their children to be taught in English. No one, of course, needs to remind a parent that his son or daughter will take the preliminary examination in English at the end of Standard VII, and that his success in that examination will determine whether or not he gets a secondary school place.

As EM classes in Nyeri County grew, Kagumo College began to train serving teachers, headmasters, and supervisors, in addition to carrying on its regular work with students in training. Over an eighteen month period from September, 1964, to February, 1966, more than twenty courses were scheduled in vacation periods. But the problems were beginning to show. The courses for teachers lasted only a week and a good sprinkling of the teachers were not P3's, but unqualified teachers who had no previous training of any kind. There were only a half-dozen supervisors for the more than 300 EM Standard I classes, and these men too needed to be trained in the principles and techniques of *New Peak*. Equipment, books, and display material were stolen from classrooms that had no locks on doors or windows. The initial purchase of equipment was itself

## The New Primary Approach / 45

a major problem, although every possible kind of economy measure was put to use. To equip a Standard I class the estimate of expense was as follows:

| | | |
|---|---|---|
| *New Peak* Texts: | Teacher's course book and a set of ten children's books | 115/20. |
| Class Equipment: | Pencils, exercise books, chalk, etc. | 60/30. |
| Apparatus: | Paste, scissors, paint brushes, etc. | 72/10. |
| | Total | 247/60. |

Thus for a class of forty, the average size, the cost was a little over 6/ per child. These estimates assumed there would be a good deal of "making do"—tobacco tins for paint palettes, bottle tops for number counters, and so on, but nevertheless there were schools in many districts that could not afford to buy the texts and the equipment in the same year. Some of the difficulty had been reduced when the Ford Foundation again stepped in, this time with a grant of £75,000 to be used over a six-year period, largely for apparatus and the travel expenses of supervisors. The grant enabled kits of apparatus to be assembled in Nairobi and sent to English Medium Standards I and II in all parts of the country.

By 1965 the term "English Medium" had been given way to "New Primary Approach," a more accurate name for what was now a national movement in the reform of primary education. The Ministry of Education reported the following number of NPA classes:

| | |
|---|---|
| Standard I | 1,920 |
| Standard II | 650 |
| Standard III | 220 |
| Standard IV | 80 |
| Standard V | 1 |

The Special Centre through the wide-ranging observations of its staff, reports from training college tutors and country supervisors, the impressions gained from teachers on in-service courses, had drawn three conclusions:

> Contrary to orthodox linguistic opinion children have not suffered any emotional disturbance as the result of learning through the medium of a foreign tongue. On the contrary they seem to be more natural and less inhibited than they used to be.
>
> Young children can develop in English a flexible command of controlled structures and vocabulary quite sufficient for their current needs both in and out of school.
>
> Given adequate preparation of the teachers and close supervision for an initial period, preferably for one year, the new course can effect a substantial improvement in the quality of the work done in African lower primary classes.[6]

A professor of education from Makerere University College in Uganda and a close student of schools in East Africa had reported a visit to an NPA class:

> The teacher was not highly qualified but very much alive and specially trained in English Medium teaching at Kagumo Training College nearby; the children had been learning English for six months. Everyone in the room seemed to be engaged; I have seldom seen children more eager to talk and learn and think. They were like little puppies on leash ready for the next exciting experience of answering in English. Hardly a word of their vernacular was spoken; the transference of meaning from experience to words was direct, fulfilling the requirement that 'the new language symbol is met in the context of the experience which it symbolizes.' The peak of the lesson was an exercise in mental arithmetic involving very simple addition of halves, quarters and units. The thinking was done in English and the answers came out in English right or wrong. The teacher queried one boy's answer, he stood in rapt recalculation, you could almost hear his brain working, 'No, it is one and a quarter, sir,' and he was right.[7]

The Ominde Commission had given the movement its enthusiastic endorsement. NPA had now gone beyond the experi-

---
[6] E. B. Castle, *Growing Up in East Africa* (London: Oxford University Press, 1966), p. 210.
[7] *Ibid.*, p. 211.

mental stage and had proven its effectiveness. It had won support from both parents and professionals, and its founders were in demand to interpret it in Uganda, China, and Zambia. *Peak* materials were in use in Singapore and Sarawak. But most important of all, P3 teachers had demonstrated that with training and supervision, books and equipment, they were able to do the job.

### Analysis and Evaluation

AND yet, in spite of this success NPA was having serious growing pains. In areas of rapid expansion it was increasingly difficult to maintain standards of training and supervision. Special Centre staff were not able to prepare courses for the upper primary grades and at the same time cope with administrative, supervisory, and training problems. The function of the training colleges and the new regional inspectors in the in-service training and supervision of teachers needed to be clarified. It was time, the Ministry of Education decided, to ask for a penetrating analysis of a program that had begun as a small experiment and had become an educational revolution.

The Ford Foundation was approached and agreed to support a study of all aspects of NPA to be undertaken by Marixius Hutasoit, formerly Secretary-General of Education and the then Deputy Minister for Planning in Indonesia, and Clifford Prator, Professor of English at the University of California in Los Angeles and a professional linguist. Messrs. Prator and Hutasoit carried out their investigation in February and March, 1965, by visiting schools in all six provinces, and conferring with teachers and officials at all levels of the educational hierarchy. Their report,[8] which was both complimentary and critical, was marked by a discussion in depth of language

---

[8] Marixius Hutasoit and Clifford H. Prator, *A Study of the "New Primary Approach" in the Schools of Kenya* (Nairobi: Ford Foundation and Ministry of Education, 1965), mimeographed.

policy issues, an evaluation of *New Peak,* and an analysis of the problems that NPA was experiencing in the field.

When the Special Centre was created in 1957 and the experiment with English Medium teaching from Standard I onwards began, Kenya was a British colony. In 1963 power was transferred to an African government, and with Independence came the Africanization of senior posts in the Ministry of Education. What would be their decision on language policy in education? Should English or Swahili or the vernacular be the medium of instruction in the early grades of the primary school? The Kenya Education Commission had made its stand clear:

> English should become the universal medium of instruction from Primary I but Kiswahili should become a compulsory subject from Primary I wherever possible. (Recommendation 48)
>
> The choice of the English medium does not mean that we wish to undermine the vernacular. The vernacular languages are essential languages of verbal communication and we recognize no difficulty in including a daily period for story-telling in the vernacular, or similar activities in the curriculum of Primary I and II. We recommend, therefore, that the vernaculars will continue to serve their historic role of providing a means of verbal communication. We see no case for assigning to them a role for which they are ill adapted, namely, the role of educational medium in the critical early years of schooling. (Paragraph 171)

With minor reservations the Prator-Hutasoit report took the same stand in advising the Ministry. The case for English was made on both social and political grounds:

> English is the greatest *lingua franca* the world has ever known; it is used by more people, of more different kinds in more widely scattered places, for more different purposes than Latin ever was. It would be absurd at this late stage of the development of mankind to regard it as the property or instrument of the small island off the coast of Europe which had the honour of giving it birth. . . .
>
> Economic development and higher living standards can be achieved only through access to science and technology. In

> today's world the language of science and technology is pre-eminently English. . . .
>
> English is equally accessible to all groups of Kenyans. It is already widely spoken in the country and well-established in the school system. Adequate materials for teaching it are available, and there are more teachers prepared to give instruction in English than in any other language. . . .
>
> The political leaders of countries as diverse as the United States, the Philippines, Ethiopia, Nigeria, Ghana, and Uganda have seen and continue to see in English one of the most effective instruments for achieving national unity. . . .
>
> Whereas Swahili, at best, permits communication within a limited area in East Africa, English is spoken by more Africans than any other tongue. . . . A Kenyan travelling abroad can win few friends and influence few people through Swahili or Kikuyu.[9]

And yet there was an important role for Swahili to play in the unification of East Africa. It is a *lingua franca* with great emotional appeal for East Africans because it is an African creation and has no taint of colonialism or capitalism. It should become a compulsory subject in the primary school curriculum beginning in Standard IV.

The report makes a strong plea for giving young Kenyans the opportunity to become "comfortably literate" in their mother tongue in primary school. One period a day in Standards I, II, and III should be given over to instruction in the vernacular and one period a week in the upper primary grades should be used to keep the earlier acquired literacy alive.

> An educational system which turned out graduates incapable of writing a readable letter home in the language of the village would be no credit to Kenya. . . . What justification can there be for denying the child the right to literacy in the mother tongue which is so much a part of his personality? We cannot believe that it is really necessary, in the name of national unity, and Pan-Africanism, to deprive African children

---

[9] Hutasoit and Prator, *op. cit.*, pp. 7–8.

of an essential part of the normal development to which children almost everywhere else in the world have easy access.[10]

The creation of new teaching materials and the development of a new methodology on NPA lines for the teaching of Swahili and the vernacular should be the function of an enlarged and reorganized Special Centre. The Centre should drop its name and become the Language Section of a new Curriculum Development Centre. Along with specialists in mathematics, science, and the other disciplines, a group of professional linguists should work out new syllabuses that would carry the spirit and practice of NPA into the upper primary grades.

As a specialist in applied linguistics and in the teaching of English as a second language, C. H. Prator put *New Peak* under critical scrutiny. His praise was generous ("on balance, the best set of materials for teaching primary level English now in use in Africa") but there were several linguistic weaknesses. The precise nature of the difficulty facing Kenya children in learning English had not been adequately diagnosed. The course had much to say about controlling the order in which grammatical structures are presented, but structural control was actually very lax; the distinction between "language patterns," "sentences," "formulas," and "conversations" was not made clear. The pupils learn quite bookish English, and teachers need more help with pronunciation problems than the series provides.

As for methodology, Prator felt there was too much reliance on the notion that in order to teach a child a second language one has only to make him want to talk about a lot of things. This is a little like saying that the best way to train a telegraph operator is to give him lots of good news to transmit without first teaching him the Morse code. More organized drill and choral work and less opportunity for uncontrolled use of language would be preferable. Some inexpensive way

---

[10] *Ibid.*, p. 14.

should be found for printing visual aids and distributing them widely rather than having each teacher make his own. And the reading of English is begun too early; it should be postponed until Standard II. There was, clearly, a need for a revision of *New Peak* and a greater use of evaluation, trial teaching in parts of the text, and a more systematic consultation with teachers and teacher trainers than had been the case in the past.

In their safaris to the provinces Prator and Hutasoit found that NPA as a program in action was tremendously popular with teachers, administrators, and parents. One parent said his children were becoming "inquisitive little devils," and a supervisor in the Western Province gave this summary of his impressions:

> The achievement of children in English Medium classes by Standard IV is much greater than that of their contemporaries in vernacular classes. Many are able to make up little stories in English after only one year of school. They have the language; their approach to solving problems is better; they are generally not shy and are ready to discuss problems with their classroom teacher without fear.[11]

It was, of course, the rapid expansion of classes that was creating serious problems. It was futile to assume that P3's, or in some cases untrained teachers, could be taught NPA theory and practice in one hasty week at a training college. Some teachers were visited by supervisors less often than once a month, and many teachers were attempting to teach under NPA methods with an inadequate supply of books and equipment. The result was a great range in the quality of teaching and learning. Some teachers spoke English with confidence, knew exactly what they wished to accomplish at each step of the course, and had well-equipped classrooms where projects of a variety of kinds were in evidence. And active children crowded around visitors to ask questions.

---

[11] *Ibid.*, p. 22.

In other classrooms English Medium instruction and NPA methods had degenerated into a sad farce:

> The model of English set by the teacher was of a type calculated to do more harm than good: "You are a pupil, isn't it?" "What did Festus found in his pocket?" "This is Margaret; he's a girl." We could not succeed in prying one audible word out of the children, who seemed turned into little masses of squirming embarrassment by our questions. . . . No pictures, no interesting objects, no real organization of activities. The textbook "had not yet arrived." The teacher went through the forms of a few of the procedures suggested in the *New Peak Course* but clearly did not understand their purposes. He allowed his pupils to spend most of their time in interminable recesses outside on the playground. The changeover to the NPA in such a class apparently amounted to no more than the replacement of good Luo by bad English.[12]

The report suggested that the Ministry should draw up and circulate widely a statement of the conditions that must be fulfilled before new NPA classes could be approved. Serving teachers should attend courses lasting a month rather than a week, and training colleges should stress the improvement of oral English. Assistant education officers needed to be trained for the supervision of NPA classes and an AEO should be responsible for not more than twenty schools. If these conditions could be met, if the "chain of command" from the Ministry to the provinces were clarified, and if foreign governments and foundations would continue to supply technical assistance then it should be possible to fix 1970 as the target date for bringing all Standard I's in Kenya under NPA.

## Research and Development

THESE then were the proposals made by Messrs. Prator and Hutasoit to the Ministry of Education. Some, but certainly not all, of their advice has been taken since the report was sub-

---

[12] *Ibid.,* p. 24.

mitted in March, 1965. The Special Centre has become the Language Section of the Curriculum Development and Research Centre. With a staff of nine it has produced a course in Swahili beginning at Standard IV, and is working on teaching materials in twelve vernaculars. The first books of *Safari,* the English course for the upper primary, have appeared after careful testing in Standard IV classrooms. The teacher who uses *Safari* is told what to do in each English period and little is left to chance. The aim for each lesson and the steps to follow, the language to be used, questions for pupils to ask each other, and even the answers to these questions are all given. Six of the ten English periods per week in Standard IV are given over to *Safari,* one is for storytelling and dramatics, and three are for supplementary reading. The level of difficulty and the African context of *Safari* may be seen in this story from the second term's work.

JANE AND THE AEROPLANE [13]

One Friday morning during the school holiday Mother said to Jane, "David's sick. He's got stomach-ache and he's crying. Go to Maria and ask her to come and see him."

Maria was Jane's aunt. She was Mother's sister, and she was younger than Mother. She was a nurse at a hospital about five miles away.

"You can stay in Maria's house tonight and come back with her tomorrow or Sunday. I hope she can come tomorrow," Mother said.

Mother went outside and caught a hen. She tied its legs together and put it in a basket. "This is a present for Maria," she said.

Soon Jane was ready. She picked up the basket and said "Goodbye!" to Mother. The road to the hospital was narrow and dusty, and there were fields on both sides. As she walked along the dusty road Jane thought about Maria. "If she's working tomorrow she'll come and see David on Sunday," she thought.

---

[13] *Safari, Children's Book I* (Nairobi: Ministry of Education, 1967), pp. 136–138. Reprinted by permission.

At about one o'clock Jane saw the hospital. It was nearly half a mile away. She started to walk more quickly.

When Jane reached the hospital she stood and looked at all the buildings. "I've forgotten where Maria's house is," Jane thought. Then she saw a man wearing a white coat. She asked him where Maria's house was. "Over there—near the airstrip," he said. He went quickly into one of the buildings.

Jane didn't know that an "airstrip" was. She walked past all the buildings. Then she came to a large flat field without any grass on it. It looked like the playground at school, but it was longer. In front of Jane there was a long line of white stones. Further away, on the other side of the field, there was another line of white stones!

Then Jane heard a noise. She looked up and saw something in the sky. It was an aeroplane! As she watched, the aeroplane seemed to get bigger. It was coming nearer! "It looks like the paper aeroplane I made at school," Jane thought.

Then the aeroplane came lower and Jane saw that it was blue and white. It had three wheels under the body. Now the aeroplane was near the ground and it came along between the two lines of white stones. The wheels touched the ground and the aeroplane went along more slowly. Then it stopped.

Jane walked along the side of the field until she was opposite the aeroplane. There were three words on the side of it. Jane read them aloud—"Flying Doctor Services." Then a man got out of the aeroplane through a door in the side. He waved to someone. Jane looked round. She saw the man in the white coat. He was walking with a nurse towards the aeroplane. Then she saw someone running towards her! It was Maria!

"Jane! Jane!" Maria shouted. "What are you doing here?"

Jane told Maria about David, then she asked, "Why has that aeroplane come here?"

"It's come to take a baby to a hospital in Nairobi. He's very sick. If he gets the right treatment quickly he'll get well again. A nurse is going to travel in the aeroplane with him," Maria said.

"Is that man a doctor?" Jane asked.

"No," Maria said. "He's the pilot. Sometimes the aeroplane brings a doctor. Sometimes, if we need some medicine very quickly we can ask a 'Flying Doctor' aeroplane to bring it. The 'Flying Doctor' aeroplanes are always very busy."

"Now I know why this field is flat. It's for aeroplanes to land on," Jane said.

"Yes, it's called an airstrip," Maria said. "The men from the village made it." Then they saw a nurse getting into the aeroplane with the baby. The pilot got in after her and then he closed the door.

Jane and Maria watched the aeroplane take off, then Maria turned to Jane. "I must go back to the hospital now," she said. "You can go to my house—it's the third one in that line of houses. I'm not working tomorrow so I'll be able to go and see David. We'll go on my bicycle. You can sit behind me."

Jane was very pleased. She liked riding on Maria's bicycle. "I'm sure Maria will make David well," she thought.

Following the very steep increase in Standard I NPA classes from 1,920 in 1965 to 2,670 in 1966 the Ministry advised sharp curtailment of new openings. A determined effort to improve supervision was mounted with the help of technical assistance from the USA. In 1964 the National Education Association of the United States, under a contract with USAID, provided five experienced primary teachers to serve as NPA supervisors. By 1967 their number had grown to ten and they were working closely with assistant education officers in visiting schools and providing in-service training to teachers in NPA methods. It is not unusual for one of these supervisors to visit five schools a day, and over the course of a month to work individually or in groups with 250 teachers. They have also been instrumental in testing new materials produced by the Curriculum Development and Research Centre. When this program of assistance phases out in 1968 and 1969 the supervisors will be replaced by Kenyan education officers.

The extent of technical assistance from abroad has been considerable. The British Government and the British Council over the years have supplied a large share of the personnel of the Special Centre and, more recently, the Language Section. Britain and Canada have sent tutors to the training colleges, and a team of Canadian teacher trainers have developed a large-scale program to upgrade serving teachers via vacation courses. And the American Teach Corps has instructed teachers and supervisors in NPA methods.

No extensive evaluation of *New Peak* has been undertaken, but the CDRC has made small-scale studies of the language competence of African children who have gone through three years of NPA classes. A study of compositions written by 300 pupils revealed a large and varied active vocabulary, but spelling was poor and these pupils did not have an adequate command of English structures. The evidence was mounting from professional linguists, from teachers and supervisors, and from the performance of the children themselves that *New Peak* needed to be thoroughly reworked, tested in the schools, and revised. It had served Kenya children well, but its weaknesses both linguistic and methodological were apparent.

What kind of balance sheet can we submit for NPA? Its faults and weaknesses are all too apparent. Both *Peak* and *New Peak* were created by a team of dedicated and intelligent educators none of whom had specialized training in linguistics. *New Peak* has its flaws, probably because it was developed too quickly by too small a staff and was not given adequate classroom testing. An evaluation of what children have learned in lower primary NPA classes has yet to be made. Whatever evaluations have been made thus far, with the exception of the studies by CDRC mentioned above, have been entirely impressionistic. When an observer sees inquiring children actively absorbed in their work he *knows* that learning is going on, but the extent and quality of that learning, the skills acquired, and the attitudes developed cannot be discovered by random observation. There is, in fact, no hard evidence by which NPA can be judged. The range in the quality of teaching and learning is probably just as wide today as it was reported to be in 1965 by Prator-Hutasoit. On the other hand, the activity methods that were once associated with NPA are now encouraged in the teaching of all subjects in the primary schools. The General Methods Section of the Curriculum Development and Research Centre has recently produced a *Book of Creative Activities* which can be used in the teaching of arithmetic, social studies, religious education, and the tribal vernaculars. Similarly, the training colleges no longer regard NPA as a separate subject related only to language teaching and now introduce their students to the theoretical underpinnings and the practical implications of learning through "activity" and "discovery."

In a determination to instruct its primary teachers explicitly in the use of texts and methods Kenya may fall into the paradox of formalizing the spirit of modern education, the essence of which surely is to set the teacher and pupil free. If NPA signalled the arrival of John Dewey in East Africa it would be a pity to see him become a dogma. On the other hand, educational theory through its own logic has seldom had any profound effect on classroom practice. It is only when theory has been built into quite specific guides for practice that it has effected wide-reaching education reforms. And this is even more true in developing countries where it is unlikely that teachers with only a limited education are going to draw from education theory their own conclusions about classroom change.

Kenya's P3 teachers appear to have proven that teachers with only a limited general education can be trained to adopt successfully techniques based on modern education concepts. Admittedly they worked in the lower primary grades where there is less demand for a general educational background. But they have demonstrated a lively intelligence, first in learning and then adopting a variety of teaching techniques and procedures. It was these and not general knowledge or "cultural background" that gave them confidence. They knew that help was available when they needed it, and that those in authority had a sympathetic understanding both of their ability and their limitations. It was under these conditions that teachers of meagre education and training were able to bring a large measure of reform and a new vitality to Kenya's primary schools.

[CHAPTER FOUR]

*The Education of Primary Teachers: Kagumo College*

It would be difficult to find any institution that has operated under greater handicaps than the Teacher Training College in East Africa. Its P3 students have "failed" to get a secondary school place, its P2's have not completed secondary school, and P1's were not selected for Form V. In his Annual Report for 1961 the principal of Kagumo College spoke of this sense of failure among his P1 group: "A few of our post-secondary school recruits enter teacher-training as a first choice, but the majority agree to join it because their other applications have been unsuccessful." Training College staffs, predominately expatriate, have suffered from turnover and mobility, and a high proportion of tutors have arrived in Kenya with no previous experience in the training of teachers. The Ministry of Education, in drawing up its annual budgets or in shaping its development plans during the colonial period, did not regard primary teacher education as a matter of high priority. Prior to Independence, the churches were encouraged to develop their own training colleges with grants from the central Government; by 1963 there were thirty-six colleges receiving aid, nineteen of which were under church or mission management. The majority of these had too small an enrollment to use specialist staff effectively. Although students were in their late teens and early twenties, the colleges, particularly those managed by the missions, gave them little social or personal freedom. And in recent years the colleges have faced the difficult task not only of providing professional training and raising the academic level of their students at the same time, but of spreading the gospel according to NPA and interpreting its principles through their own teaching methods. In the face of all of these problems, the astonishing fact is that the colleges have done so much with so little.

The Cinderella days may now be over. The Revised Development Plan 1965–70 recognizes the need to improve the quality of primary education by upgrading the qualifications of teachers. By 1970 the annual output of the training colleges will rise to 2,900 with a trebling, it is hoped, of the number of P1 trainees. The thirty-four colleges of 1965 will be reduced to fifteen with the expectation that these will increase both in enrollment and efficiency. And a massive program of vacation course training designed to upgrade serving teachers has been organized in the colleges by the Kenya Institute of Education. Some of these changes are evident at Kagumo, now a well-established college that began training teachers in 1944.

### Kagumo College

At 5,600 feet, Kagumo lies on the spine of a ridge in the foothills of the Aberdares and within view of Mount Kenya. The hillsides of this area, 90 miles from Nairobi and 6 from Nyeri, are divided into 6- or 8-acre *shambas* of bananas, maize, beans, and coffee, and in altitudes of 7,000 feet or more, tea. Thatched huts dot the sides of the ridges in clumps of three or four with here and there a tin roof signalling comparative wealth and status. Families and clans live together, but the village as a unit of organization is rare in this part of East Africa. In Nyeri County the standard of living is higher than in many parts of Kenya because the rainfall is adequate and the Kikuyu, an energetic and intelligent tribe, now produce cash crops. Fifteen years ago this was the scene of Mau Mau troubles. The bitterness of the Emergency period has largely disappeared and Europeans and the Kikuyu have forgiven, if not forgotten, the atrocities that were perpetrated by all parties to the struggle. Scars, of course, still remain, and the headmaster of one of Kagumo's teaching practice schools had his career interrupted for eight years when the British locked him into a detention camp.

## Student Life

KAGUMO's 300 students come from all parts of Kenya for a two-year course. P1's, P2's, and P3's are, in the main, taught separately in class groups of twenty-five. In making its selection of students, the college gives P3 and P2 candidates entrance tests in English comprehension and mathematics, and interviews whenever possible. As indicated above, selection of P3's is now made from a larger number of applicants than in previous years. In 1967, seventy-five P2's were chosen from 475 applicants and the academic standing of P1 candidates has clearly improved in the last five years. Kagumo students pay no tuition fees and are given clothing and pocket-money allowances. Their board and transportation costs are also paid by the college.

Kagumo probably has more amenities than a secondary school. Study-bedrooms shared by two students have almost entirely replaced the old dormitories in which twenty beds were crowded together. The library is large and well used; there is no dearth of playing fields and the men's common room is equipped with TV. Co-education, which was introduced with some apprehension in 1965, appears to be fully accepted, although the high wire fence which in that year was built around the women's residence quadrangle is still standing. All the buildings are of stone or cinder block, one story high, and are grouped in quadrangles. The only really attractive aspects of the college compound are the avenues of tall jacaranda trees which turn into mists of purple in October and

November. Students appear to have accepted the limitations of the college budget in two important respects: the allowance for meals of 2/ per student per day, and no hot water for washing themselves or their clothes.

The tension between freedom and restriction for students is resolved in different ways at the various training colleges depending to a considerable extent on whether traditions were established by the missions. Kagumo is a nonsectarian college and has no church affiliation. Its students have more freedom than those in Roman Catholic training colleges, but less than those in some other nonsectarian colleges. All students are required to attend morning assembly, and seven periods of classes each day. They play games in the afternoon, study for an hour or more at organized prep every evening, and turn out their lights at 10:30. They are not entirely free to come and go as they please on week ends. The restrictions are in fact similar to those of the secondary schools, but Kagumo students are older, of course, and a good many of the P3's taught for several years as unqualified teachers before entering the college. Kagumo recognizes the maturity of its students by giving them freedom to manage the various clubs and societies and organize a good share of the games, but in other respects there is little of the freedom or the responsibility that usually goes with life in a college. The Ominde Commission was exercised on this point and recommended that training colleges should create conditions favoring maturity and responsibility:

> A training college for teachers is an institution for students who, in a very short while, will be independent men and women responsible for children in schools. It is essential that a student, at whatever level, on reaching a training college, should be aware that he is entering a community of young adults and entitled to the freedom and status of that condition. This change of status between school and college is particularly important for women students, who must learn to stand on their own feet, for very shortly they may find themselves posted as the only woman teacher in a school. Training colleges have, unfortunately, inherited memories of earlier associ-

ations with intermediate schools, out of which many of them sprang, and although a fully adult atmosphere, in which responsibility and self-control are fostered, now exists in many colleges, yet in others some residue of the old, restrictive, protective atmosphere still seems to cling. This cramping spirit retards growth towards responsible maturity and at the same time it hinders recruitment, for as long as young people, on leaving school, associate training colleges with the controls and atmosphere of a school, they will be inclined to plan their future in other fields.[1]

## Expatriate and African Staff

THE principal of Kagumo until recently was Alexander Getao, an Old Boy of Alliance who was trained for teaching at Makerere, later studied in Britain, and came to Kagumo in 1964. One of his most serious problems was to hold on to his staff. In 1965 he weathered a 70 per cent staff turnover and a year later eight of his staff were posted to other colleges or returned to their home countries. Turnover must, of course, be accepted when the majority of tutors are expatriates on two-or four-year contracts. But African staff (in 1967 there were eight Africans in a teaching staff of nineteen) are almost equally mobile as the Ministry posts them to other colleges, the inspectorate, or CDRC. But this is not a new problem for Kagumo; in 1959 the entire English Department disappeared to other posts, other countries, or on long (four-month) leave to which an expatriate tutor is entitled after two years of service. And no one who was on the college staff in 1961 was on the scene five years later.

Expatriate staff are usually experienced teachers with high academic qualifications, but frequently they have had no experience in teacher education and are innocent of primary school methods. When they arrive in Kenya they need to make the "cultural leap," and learn the difficulties that face primary

---

[1] *Kenya Education Commission Report, Part I*, para. 345.

school leavers who are in training to become primary school teachers and to whom English is a second language. If they are intelligent, impervious to frustration, and genuinely committed to doing a good job they will succeed—as were six Canadians, four Englishmen, and one American at Kagumo in 1967. The need for expatriate tutors will continue for some years and the Ministry of Education in 1967 made an unabashed plea to teachers in a number of countries abroad:

> Would you like to participate in an interesting, enriching, and rewarding experience that will add significantly to your life? Have you ever thought about the possibility of living and working abroad? Are you interested in, and anxious to learn about the peoples, cultures, and educational systems of other countries? Are you flexible, adaptable and able to adjust to an environment in many ways similar, yet in some ways different from your own? If so, and if you are a well-qualified and experienced teacher, then an unusual opportunity awaits you—in Kenya.[2]

At the same time the Ministry was recruiting Kenya citizens who were returning from universities abroad and upgrading the qualifications of tutors already on the job. To "localize" training college staffs with graduates was proving to be a slow process: by 1967 only twenty-nine Kenya citizen graduates had accepted tutorships, while the number of expatriate graduate tutors stood at 154. If the training colleges are to foster a sense of national unity among their students and imbue them with a belief that they can, through teaching, develop a healthy sense of loyalty and nationhood in primary school children, African rather than expatriate tutors will be more effective. A tutor needs, however, to have been a primary school teacher at some stage in his life and at the moment Kenya is searching for a channel through which an experienced and successful P1 teacher can leave the classroom, enter the University of East Africa to improve himself academically and professionally, and

---

[2] *Teacher Education Bulletin* (Nairobi: Equatorial Publishers, 1967), p. 80.

then, as a graduate, join the staff of a training college. Until this channel is opened by modifying present admission requirements of the university, the flow into the colleges of African tutors with adequate qualifications will remain but a trickle.

## A Crowded Curriculum

THE latest published version of the curriculum in use at Kagumo lists seventeen subjects taken by P3 students over the two-year course. All subjects taught in the primary school are included, and in each course two-thirds of the time is devoted to improving the student's academic background and one-third to methods and materials. In addition to the primary syllabus subjects, the curriculum includes education, blackboard writing, and English methods. Mathematics and English are given 30 per cent of class time over the two-year period. This pattern of subjects has been typical of all the training colleges but change is in the air and the Kenya Institute of Education has recently recommended a major reform. The Institute, an ingenious device imported from Britain, is a partnership formed between a university and a group of training colleges for the purpose of maintaining the academic and professional standards of the colleges. In Kenya the University College at Nairobi has only recently begun to train teachers, and the Institute has been more a partnership between the Ministry (the dominant partner) and the colleges.

The proposal is to set aside a block of twelve periods a week, roughly one-third of class time, for a comprehensive education course and to devote all the remaining time to upgrading the student's academic background. The education block will be organized by one tutor with the assistance of several colleagues. The emphasis will be on preparation for lower primary teaching and topics should include:

Child study
Learning theory
Teaching methods in language, reading, number, and handwriting
Teaching aids
School organization and management

Here, of course, is one of the basic dilemmas of the training college. How is it possible to prepare the P3 student theoretically and practically for the craft of teaching, and at the same time teach him more English and history and eight other subjects? The colleges can do one but not both of these tasks well, and if they are to be essentially training enterprises, they cannot at the same time be secondary schools.

The proposed education courses raise another fundamental question: are the colleges going to continue to be relatively autonomous as in the past, deciding their own syllabus in each subject, and setting their own examinations within a framework of advice given by the Institute? Or are they going to become creatures of the Ministry following prescribed syllabuses and preparing their students for common examinations? There are persuasive arguments on both sides. Given the present turnover of tutors, their lack of experience in primary teacher training, and their innocence at the beginning of their contract on such matters as NPA and language difficulties, a common syllabus is necessary as a guide or as a frame in which to teach. Expatriate tutors would then not make up their own courses, and when they leave, a recognized syllabus would ensure some degree of continuity. Furthermore, as with secondary education, a common syllabus and external examinations are means of keeping academic and professional standards at an acceptable level. But herein lies a danger: external examinations could create a climate of cramming, and instead of producing mature adults the colleges might turn out schoolboys. If the colleges are required to conform they will lose their present individuality and uniqueness, and those principals who are attempting to create an atmosphere of greater freedom and responsibility will be frustrated. Standards in a number of colleges do, however, need to be raised and whether this can be done without destroying the benefits that go with diversity and autonomy is the problem. Common syllabuses but not external examinations may be the best solution.

### Teaching Practice

ALL of a Kagumo student's time is not of course spent in college classrooms. In four of the six terms the students go out to nearby schools for three weeks of teaching practice. Women students continue to live at the college but men move into teachers' houses on primary school compounds and take all provisions and equipment with them. Through a minor miracle of organization, each group of students assigned to a particular school are provided with dishes, cutlery, cooking utensils, buckets, an ironing board, and a lantern—all listed and boxed —at the beginning of each teaching period. Students are given money to buy their food (3/ per day) and they are then deposited by school bus, fully stocked and equipped at schools that may be up to 25 miles from the college. As the students take over their classes, the regular teachers tend to disappear or go on vacation and, surprisingly, are not asked to supervise or assist the students. The only supervision is given by the Kagumo staff who follow the students into the schools and observe them as much as time permits.

Once a year the Institute of Education sends a team or panel composed of inspectors, tutors from other colleges, and Ministry Officials to inspect Kagumo students while on teaching practice. The following excerpts are from a sketch [3] written by the author, who served on the Kagumo panel in November, 1965:

---

[3] "Safari in the Short Rains," *Wesleyan University Alumnus*, LI (November, 1966), pp. 11–15. Reprinted by permission.

## Education of Primary Teachers: Kagumo College / 67

The instructions were clear enough: rendezvous at Kagumo at 8:30 and drive out to the schools with the college tutors. Among the earliest to arrive was the secretary of the group, a well-tanned Englishman perhaps 55 or a bit under, in full safari outfit: a belted bush shirt with matching khaki shorts, knee socks and heavy brogues. All very serviceable and official we thought, but perhaps rather too vivid a reminder of colonial days. This was Kenya two years after Independence, and the leader of the party was the Chief Inspector of Schools, a young African in a dark business suit, carrying a pair of gum boots in case his car had trouble on roads now soggy after two weeks of rain. College tutors bustled about with lists of students, thermoses of coffee, box lunches and roughly drawn maps. Within 15 minutes Land Rovers, Peugeots, VW's and even a Mercedes were moving off the college compound and over the red murram roads to the primary schools of Nyeri District, 50 miles from the Equator but blessedly cool at altitudes of 5,000 feet or more.

Within a mile of the college the Mercedes sank to its hubs in a pool that fully covered the narrow road. The British tutor, whose car it was, explained that he had brought it back on his last leave and it was usually very good in mud, but today he should have put on his chains. Before he could become further flustered bare-foot boys began to spring out of the bush like djinns and to push from all sides. The road now wound through valleys of brilliant green and across streams choked with grey and white water. Each time the Mercedes came to a bridge of planks the tutor stopped, said he really ought to get out and inspect, but took a chance and drove slowly over.

The first primary school was high on a ridge, but the playground was level and on it two classes were running a relay race. Several student teachers, lesson books in hand, watched the car stop and the visitors get out. They seemed anxious to get their ordeal over and led their examiners to their classrooms explaining hurriedly the subject of the next lesson. David, one of the student teachers, had written the aim of the lesson in his notebook: "To elicit coal fields in Great Britain and industries near them." His college tutors had obviously persuaded him of the advantages of visual aids for he proudly unfurled a home-made map of Great Britain showing the major coal fields, and their nearby cities. He then produced from an aluminum pail a seemingly endless supply of objects from sticking plaster to a transistor radio and followed this with pictures of still more objects. When the class was satisfied that these were some of the things that British factories made, David proceeded to pin rectangular cards on his map, each card carrying a symbol of the article manufactured in each city. All this was done with great vigor and David was obviously determined both to tell and show his class what he wanted them to know. But in his enthusiasm he forgot to "elicit the coal fields" and when the lesson ended the children knew that knives and forks came from Sheffield and ships from Glasgow, but not much more.

Like most teachers whether old or young, student teachers talk too much. One young man delivered a forty-minute lecture on Christopher Columbus and encouraged "class participation" in a curious way. He would say, for example, "Christopher Columbus visited Portugal." Then he would repeat the line except for the last word and the class would supply "Portugal" in chorus. Similarly, when Columbus was having his troubles with a dispirited crew: "We are going forward. We are going . . ." And the class roared its word of assurance. Both the lecture and the chorused responses were disconcerting to the children in adjoining classrooms. Partitions between the rooms are only six or seven feet high and the space above is unenclosed. Thus it is quite easy for children to hear three teachers almost equally well, and the astonishing thing is that they have learned to filter out the other two and concentrate on their own.

After two days of examining 102 students in 28 schools, the team returned to the college for an afternoon with the Kagumo staff. Seated around native wood tables in the college library they compared grades and carefully observed the British tradition of understating a student's performance. The highest grade was B— and only one student achieved that distinction. On the other hand, no one failed, and the large majority were given respectable C's. The examiners reported their marks but the college staff decided the final grades.

The dialogue between examiners and staff was a friendly exchange of shop talk with the Chief Inspector steering the discussion towards generalizations on the students' teaching performance. These ranged from comments on the use of the blackboard to a plea that if independent judgment and critical thinking were to be nurtured in Kenya schools they would have to take root first in the training colleges. Throughout this discussion the college staff aptly defended itself and reminded their guests of the guaranteed imperfections of the student teacher. For nearly three hours the conversation continued as it does every year when the examiners make their call. Colleges are not openly compared but each knows that it is being judged comparatively and if its standards are slipping it will be told so, and each college realizes that somebody cares, that while it may be miles off in the *bundu* and in apparent isolation, the Institute and the Ministry are concerned enough to send a team of assessors to chivy it out of the ruts of complacency or despair and politely insist that it reach for excellence.

When the meeting adjourned for tea everyone seemed surprised that it wasn't raining. It was now the middle of the short rains and Kagumo hadn't had a shower for two days.

## Model Schools and Teacher Upgrading

KAGUMO has been a pioneer in the NPA movement. As early as 1962 one of its tutors initiated three English Medium Standard I classes in nearby primary schools and in the same year the Special Centre set up a one-week course at Kagumo for training college tutors in NPA methods. As we have seen in Chapter Three, NPA classes spread quickly in Nyeri County under the supervision of Millo Shaw. As a further means of interpreting and demonstrating what NPA really is, Kagumo has recently acquired a model school. This is not a new or in any way a special school but simply the primary school of Kagumo Location, half a mile from the college. The college, the county education officer, and the Headmaster have reached an agreement concerning staffing, purchase of equipment, and the renovation of several classrooms.

The model school idea was suggested by Prator and Hutasoit, although the term they used was "NPA Centre." The college will use such a centre or school for demonstration purposes and will show its students in training just what NPA means in action at all levels of the primary school when staff, buildings, equipment, and textbooks are at an acceptable standard. The school can also be used for demonstration purposes when serving teachers are taking courses at the college. Further, it will test new materials developed by the CDRC. To serve these functions the model schools (in time one will be attached to each training college) will be typical primary schools but staffed and equipped better than most. All the staff will be trained teachers paid on the normal salary scale. Classrooms will be fully equipped with texts and apparatus, and these will be safely stored behind locked doors and windows. Renovations will be made to classrooms so that twenty-five college students seated on verandahs can see and hear what is going on. The classrooms themselves will be suitably equipped with blackboards and bulletin boards. The equipment will be financed from the Ford Foundation grant, and it is expected that construction costs will be underwritten by a foreign donor. Meanwhile, the Kagumo Primary School and the college have already entered into a new relationship, the school classrooms now have cement floors and are better equipped and demonstration lessons have begun.

In 1965 two representatives of the Canadian Government toured East Africa inquiring from each of the three Governments in what way Canada might assist them in educational development. Kenya suggested several priorities but high on the list was the upgrading of primary school teachers. Within a year a team of five highly qualified masters from Canadian teachers colleges were in Nairobi as a part of the staff of the Kenya Institute of Education. Their task was to plan in-service courses on a massive scale using all training college facilities during vacation periods, and to start with two groups— headmasters and unqualified teachers with four or more years of experience. The team gave itself a rapid and intensive orientation to primary and teacher education in Kenya and then prepared syllabuses and made the necessary administrative

## Education of Primary Teachers: Kagumo College / 71

arrangements for the first courses. Quite incredibly, these courses opened in December, 1966, with 500 headmasters and 1,800 unqualified teachers in residence at twenty-five colleges. The courses lasted one week and marked the beginning of an integrated plan for improving the competence and morale of both groups.

The emphasis of this scheme in its first year was professional and methodological, and no attempt was made to improve academic qualifications. The heads studied child development, discussed ways of assisting and supervising their staff, and were brought up-to-date on new ideas and techniques in teaching primary school subjects. The approach to unqualified teachers was practical and explicit with instruction in the use of activity methods in several subjects and demonstrations of techniques in teaching *New Peak* and *Safari* courses. Every effort was made to show the heads and the UT's both the "why" and the "how" of modern primary methods. The courses were given during the school holidays in December, April, and August, and training college tutors formed the staff. Tutors have experimented with different teaching techniques: demonstration lessons, large group lectures, panel discussion, and radio broadcasts. Radio programs were specially prepared by the School Broadcasting Division of the Voice of Kenya and broadcasts included one on "The Activity Program in the Lower Primary" and four on the teaching of reading. Frequently the broadcasts carried a recording of a demonstration lesson. Leaving nothing to chance, the Canadian team not only prepared the broadcasts but provided notes for tutors on how to make the most of them by discussion in advance and follow-up.

Between the vacation courses there was a series of eight radio broadcasts, mainly on child study, and two written assignments. Each headmaster was given the option of writing on several topics, one of which asked him to outline a problem in staff relations that he encountered during the year, and to describe his method of handling it. The teachers were required to outline the main features of NPA as they applied to the teaching of English in lower primary classes. The sequence of vacation courses in which radio broadcasts were integrated with daily teaching, the follow-up by radio and correspondence work, and the massive scale of the enterprise were all clearly experimental. Experience to date indicates that two- or three-week courses twice a year would probably be preferable to the present plan, and these should be followed by academic courses in which the more ambitious unqualified teachers could prepare to write Kenya Junior School Certificate examinations in two or three subjects. This may be done through an integration of vacation courses, radio, and correspondence.

The program reveals that Kenya is no longer prepared to tolerate large numbers of primary school leavers with no training continuing to teach in the primary schools. Those with one or two years of experience will be expected to enrol for the two-year course in the training colleges and those with longer experience are now required to take the sequence of courses described above and upgrade themselves to P3 status or better. The program also reflects both the assumption that the bulk of Kenya's primary teaching force for some years to come will consist of P3 teachers, and the conviction that teachers with a meagre education can be trained to teach effectively by modern standards.

Kagumo and the other training colleges are therefore busy the year round and the demands on tutors are considerable. The colleges appear to have a new sense of purpose and a firmer understanding of their role. For this, the Institute of Education must be given most of the credit. Through its teams of assessors, subject panels, and in-service training programs the Institute has raised both the academic and professional standards of the training colleges and has demonstrated that the colleges can be effective instruments for improving the quality of primary education. The problems related to student morale and motivation, staff inexperience and turnover, autonomy or tighter control will continue to worry college principals and their staffs, but within a different context. The days of isolation and neglect are over, and the training colleges are now fully within the main stream of a national concern to improve the qualifications and the competence of primary teachers.

**PART THREE. SECONDARY EDUCATION**

[CHAPTER FIVE]

## Schools in Transition

### The Rule of Cambridge

THE marked increase in the number of careers open to Africans in the years just prior to Independence was mentioned in Chapter One. By 1963 a boy or girl with a Division I or a good Division II school certificate had a wide range of choices. He could enter the Sixth Form and possibly go on to university, or find his way on scholarship to an American college; he could enroll for training courses in one of several government departments, a public utility, or a business firm. And with so many opportunities teaching lost much of its earlier appeal. With a university degree his starting salary in the civil service or private enterprise would be between £800 and £1,000 a year and if he completed a diploma course he might begin at £500 to £700. The differences between these salaries and the annual pay of the laborer (£80) or average cash income (£20) of the peasant farmer was enormous. No wonder then that the competition to enter a secondary school was so keen and the practice of cramming so prevalent. It was not only a matter of securing a school certificate; a First Division would open many more doors.

When the Ominde Commission began its inquiry it found a "popular clamour" for secondary education rising from most parts of the country. The increasing number of pupils completing primary school and the need for educated African manpower did much to account for this growing demand. "Cambridge" was replacing the KPE as the watershed of personal advancement. Access to a secondary schoool and the winning of a Cambridge Overseas School Certificate became a passionate longing in the hearts of thousands of primary school leavers. The anxieties of teachers and students over examination results had profound effects on secondary education. A grim adherence to the syllabus, the working over of old examination papers, and the memorization of dictated notes all became familiar routines. The choice of subjects in most schools was narrow, and practical or vocational subjects had not yet found a place in the curriculum. The Commission urged both a loosening up of the curriculum and a more imaginative kind of teaching.

> What we need to do is to break with the socially conditioned academic tradition of our schools and to give our children, each according to his ability, a well-rounded education of mind and hand and character. Even within the so-called academic subjects themselves we would like to see every effort made to relate them in a practical way to the actual real world. . . .
>
> We seek a freer access for the practical subjects to the charmed circle of secondary education and a less purely bookish approach to all subjects. . . . We also wish to emphasize that most difficult task of education—the development of a power to think and do things for yourself. In this connection, the Cambridge School Certificate is a real enemy, for it is entirely possible to pass in subjects merely by amassing knowledge, cramming book-learning that has little educational significance in itself, except perhaps as a training of the memory.[1]

Attacks on the "real enemy" came from several quarters in the next five years. Agriculture and industrial arts had been introduced in 1960 at Chavakali, the first *harambee* day secondary school. These, along with domestic science and commercial subjects, gained added recognition when officials of the World Bank stipulated in 1966 that facilities for teaching at

---

[1] *Kenya Education Commission Report, Part I*, p. 69.

least one of these subjects should be provided in all schools to be built with International Development Association loan funds. As a later chapter on Chavakali reveals, the teaching of agriculture expanded under the Vocational Agriculture Project financed by the United States Agency for International Development, and since 1963 "Agriculture: Principles and Practices" has been a Cambridge examination option.

An East African Examinations Council was formed in 1967 to conduct within East Africa "such academic, technical and other examinations as the Council may consider necessary or desirable in the public interest." The three governments, the university, and the Cambridge Syndicate are represented on the council, and probably within the next few years school certificate examinations will be set and marked in East Africa. "Cambridge" will then come to an end.

Critics of the Cambridge examinations have usually directed their attacks against the wrong enemy. The Cambridge Syndicate has offered African schools carefully designed examination papers, a highly competent system of marking, and a willingness to adopt new syllabuses more closely related to African conditions. The real enemy was not really Cambridge at all but the miserable methods of teaching and learning that developed in the desperate attempts of students to pass "School Cert." In a period of rapid expansion and high teacher turnover (fourth-year students might have as many as a dozen English teachers between Form I and Form IV) the Cambridge examinations provided a needed constant, a permanent frame in which teachers and students knew what had to be taught. Without this frame or context secondary education would have become chaos in which new and inexperienced teachers attempted to create their own courses. Furthermore, the skillful and creative teacher was never severely limited by the examination system. Once he had won the confidence of his students he could prepare them for school certificate and carry them well beyond the prescribed syllabus.

## Curriculum Change

BEGINNINGS have been made, usually with the marked cooperation of the Cambridge Syndicate, to change the syllabus in several subjects. An example is Nuffield physics. The Nuffield Science Teaching Project began its work in Britain in 1962 when teachers and educational organizations felt a need to discover more effective and imaginative ways of teaching science. The aim was to develop materials that would help teachers to present science in "a more lively, exciting and intelligible way." British teachers who participated in the project are now in Kenya and in December, 1970, students who have followed the physics course will sit for the first Nuffield Physics School Certificate examination. As an example of the new approach, here is a question that appeared on a Nuffield O-level physics paper in England in 1966:

> A number of people are sitting by the side of a large lake, watching a girl skiing on the water, towed by a speed boat. Someone asks 'What keeps her up?' Five answers are given to this question.
>
> (a) 'The water is at atmospheric pressure, and this pressure keeps her up.'
> (b) 'It's a displacement effect. She sinks a little and this produces an upthrust equal to the weight of water displaced. This keeps her up.'
> (c) 'It's like a rifle bullet. She travels so fast she doesn't have time to sink.'
> (d) 'She places herself so that the skis slope upwards at the front, and then the water has an upwards force. This supports her weight.'
> (e) 'It's a Bernoulli effect. Water rushes under the skis, and because it is moving faster the pressure is greater, and this keeps her up.'
>
> Comment on each of these answers, giving the reasons why you consider some to be entirely wrong, and assessing the degree of truth in the others.

Give a more detailed explanation on the lines of the answer you consider to be most satisfactory. Illustrate your answer with diagrams if you think they would help. Say why the girl sinks if the boat stops.

The catalysts in what has become widespread curriculum change are the staff of the Curriculum Development and Research Centre. The "new" mathematics and science curriculums that have emerged in the United States and Europe are well known in Kenya. A Science Teaching Centre opened in Nairobi in 1961 with a grant from the Ford Foundation. Its objective was to help teachers learn more science and more effective ways of teaching it through in-service courses, the preparation of schemes of work and courses of study, and through the use of a lending library of science texts and reference works. The Science Centre has now become the Science Section of CDRC and its staff are at work with teachers who are trying out Nuffield physics and chemistry courses, and exploring ways of building inexpensive apparatus. The Section is also cooperating with Unesco's biology project through which courses will emerge that are appropriate for tropical Africa. New courses are being developed and tested, and courses for teachers using the draft series of the East African Schools Mathematics Project are held regularly during vacation periods. In a program designed to improve the teaching of English the Language Section of CDRC works with the inspectorate in what has now become a familiar pattern for Centre staff: the production of new teaching materials, e.g. *The Teaching of Idiom;* experimentation with the materials in the schools; and in-service training of teachers. When the materials have been adequately tested they are revised and rewritten by the specialists in each section and then printed for distribution to the schools. Centre staff not only train experienced teachers in the use of the new materials, but work closely with tutors and students in the training colleges.

The objective is to create a partnership of specialists, teachers, and training college tutors who work together on the tasks of curriculum change. And as new materials are written, tested, and produced, a classroom methodology appropriate to the new content is developed and demonstrated. This may be the means of changing the ethos of a school system away from passivity and cramming towards inquiry, discovery, and self-reliance. In the days of what used to be known as progressive education teachers were asked to accept a new theory of education and were then expected to find ways of putting the theory to work in the classroom. The new approach stemming from curriculum development centres in all parts of the world is to offer teachers a choice to participate with specialists in developing new content and method, and as these are tested and adopted, they become the vehicle on which new educational theory rides into the classroom.

## *Harambee*

PRIOR to Independence the typical African secondary school was residential and modestly equipped with classrooms, laboratories, dormitories, and playing fields. The staff, the large majority of whom were expatriates, lived in comfortable and sturdy houses on the outskirts of the compound. When the pressure for more places began to mount, and the maintained school system could no longer satisfy the national hunger for secondary education, local communities began to open *harambee* or self-help schools. By 1965 well over 100 of these day schools were in operation. Typically, local leaders secured sufficient contributions in money and labor to renovate an existing primary or former intermediate school, and parents somehow managed to come forward with fees ranging from 500/ to 1,000/ a year. Teachers were usually found by raiding primary schools.

Judged by the usual criteria of staff qualifications, buildings, and equipment, these schools gave little promise of maintaining even minimum standards of secondary education. But at a time when fewer than 10 per cent of primary school leavers could be admitted to maintained secondary schools, the opening of *harambee* schools was, from a political point of view, little short of providential. In 1965 they accounted for nearly half of all Form I places. By other criteria they were a mixed blessing. Following a study of the schools in several parts of the country, the Ominde Commission was "much disturbed by the probability that many of the children in these schools would not in fact receive an education that would justify the description of secondary." They found, for example, that the schools were understaffed, had no prospect of employing graduates, and were forced to rely on P1 teachers. Classes were large, frequently forty-five to fifty, and facilities were poor. No *harambee* school visited by the Commission had a laboratory. And yet, in spite of these dire warnings self-help schools have continued to open, and to flourish; by 1967 the schools of *harambee* origin outnumbered the aided schools of the state system.

## Secondary Expansion

THE Kenya Government has been well aware of the "popular clamour" and has recognized the need to expand secondary education. At the beginning of the 1965 school year sixty-five new Forms I were opened in maintained schools and a development plan for further expansion was taking shape. *The Revised Development Plan 1966–70* placed high priority on the expansion of secondary schools, technical and trade schools, and training colleges. The highlights of the education section of the plan were these:

> The number of students in aided *secondary schools* would *double* between 1965 and 1970.
> Sixth Form enrollments would *treble* and fees at this level would be abolished.

New *secondary trade and technical schools* would be built and for every 100 students in such schools in 1965 there would be 184 in 1970.

The number of *secondary school teachers* would increase from 1,700 to 2,950 through new training programs and the employment of expatriate teachers.

To finance a development program as ambitious as this Kenya needed external aid. In 1966 the Government negotiated a loan of some £2½ million with the International Development Association to cover 70 per cent of construction and equipment costs of the first (1965–1967) phase of the plan. Britain contributed a former army installation, the largest ever built in the Commonwealth, and helped to convert it into a secondary school and training college. Sweden offered to build, equip, and staff a college for the training of secondary science teachers, and the United States undertook to assist the Kenya Polytechnic so that it could almost double its enrollment in the plan period. All of this assistance was welcome but the rapid growth of secondary education has left Kenya with a crushing burden of recurrent expenditure which in 1967 exceeded £3 million for secondary schools alone.

## *Staffing*

WHEN secondary school enrollment almost trebles [2] in less than five years, the problem of staffing becomes acute. Kenya has been fortunate in attracting teachers from abroad at a time when few qualified African teachers were available. Britain has continued to be the most productive source of supply and in 1967 alone more than 100 graduate teachers were recruited through the Ministry of Overseas Development and the British Graduate Volunteer Programme. In recent years Kenya has made bilateral agreements with several countries as a means of

---

[2] Total enrollment in maintained, assisted, and unaided secondary schools rose from 30,120 in 1963 to 88,779 in 1967.

increasing the expatriate teacher supply. In 1961 the Teachers for East Africa program was launched and over the next six years it sent some 800 trained American and British teachers to Kenya, Tanzania, and Uganda. As American participation in TEA phased out, the Peace Corps began to arrive and by 1967 there were 140 volunteers teaching in Kenya on two-year contracts. Canada was by then becoming a major source, and other participating countries included Australia, Denmark, France, New Zealand, and West Germany.

But Kenya is attempting to reduce the proportion (70 per cent in 1967) of noncitizens in the teaching force of the aided secondary schools. The Department of Education of University College, Nairobi, is now producing graduate teachers through both an undergraduate and a graduate education course, and some 300 nongraduate teachers will complete the SI course in 1968 at Kenyatta College and the new Kenya Science Teachers College. It will, however, be well into the seventies before secondary school teachers are Kenyanized. In the meantime, expatriates will be needed, particularly to maintain an appropriate proportion of graduate teachers; in the recent years of rapid expansion that proportion has fallen to close to 50 per cent.

## Desegregation

SEGREGATION on racial lines in all secondary schools officially ended in 1963. African girls and boys did not, however, immediately pour into the former European and Asian schools, largely because of the high level of fees. For reasons that can be traced to their founding as Kenya versions of British public schools, the European schools were comparatively expensive to maintain. Almost all of the staff were graduates and thus salary costs were high; buildings and grounds were on a more generous scale than at African schools, and a more varied European diet accounted for higher food bills. Their fees were in some cases seven times those charged in African schools and well beyond the reach of most African parents.

The Ominde Commission explored this problem in considerable detail and came out strongly in favor of a unified and integrated system of schools with a uniform fee structure. This would, of course, have to be a long-term objective because any immediate and major reduction of fees would damage the quality and efficiency of the former European schools. Some economies could, however, be achieved by reducing administrative, maintenance, and food costs, while African schools should be allowed somewhat larger budgets, particularly for food, which in most African schools was only 1/50 per pupil per day. Meanwhile, as these efforts to equalize costs were going forward, the Commission recommended that the doors to the high-cost schools should be opened wider to able and needy African students through a system of Government bursaries. By 1967 African boys and girls accounted for half the intake of all former European and Asian secondary schools, and 1,100 Africans enrolled in those schools were receiving bursaries. Thus desegregation has been achieved, but full integration will come more slowly as the next chapter reveals.

[CHAPTER SIX]

## A Former European School: Kenya High

### Monument and Memorial

KENYA High School has been variously described as one of the six great schools of the Commonwealth, the Cheltenham of Kenya, and the "heifer *boma.*" On its 160 acres of lawn, woods, and playing fields which overlook the Kileleshwa Valley a few miles from the centre of Nairobi, the traditions of a British public school are everywhere in evidence: girls wear white shirts, striped ties, and grey skirts and live in houses presided over by a housemistress-matron. At meals a pair of plaques in the dining hall remind them of the British universities Old Girls have entered, and games are compulsory two afternoons a week after tea.

No secondary school in Kenya can match it in facilities and amenities. When the institution was officially completed, the Colonial Government had spent some £700,000 on stone buildings roofed with red tiles and able to accommodate 500 boarders and 100 day girls. Ten houses stretch in a semicircle around a 5-acre plot; classrooms form their own quadrangle and beyond them stand eight science laboratories and a lecture theatre. Between the tuition and residence blocks are the dining hall and the administration centre, and on the periphery are twenty tennis courts, six hockey pitches, and a terraced outdoor theatre. But the generosity of Government was not sufficient to complete the school and in later years private subscriptions have built a swimming pool, chapel, and library.

Kenya has no more magnificent monument to the faith of the European community that it had come to Kenya to stay. Immediately after World War II upcountry settlers and Nairobi businessmen began to chafe at the conditions under which their daughters went to school. Kenya High had been founded in 1930 with ninety girls and by 1945 had grown to an enrollment of 330. It occupied the upper floor of the Nairobi Primary School but its residences were scattered in several locations. The majority of the boarders were housed in temporary military hutments with bucket latrines, tin baths, and an inadequate water supply. At intervals throughout 1946 and 1947 letters appeared in the Nairobi press and one settler mother after commenting on the "scandalous conditions the girls and staff are called upon to endure" made her plea:

> Remember these girls are the future mothers of Kenya; they can do more to lead the African into a better understanding of life than a man can as they are fundamentally better fitted for welfare work. Therefore it is essential that they should live under highest civilized conditions during these impressionable years and be given the finest education possible . . . and the pick of the teaching profession, which is only possible if these teachers are provided with the amenities of life. . . .
>
> Surely we as Settlers and parents who are the backbone of Kenya are entitled to assure that our money is not laid out on super Government offices but that the first building to be erected will be a decent, hygienic building to house our Kenya High School girls.[1]

In 1946 the Government's estimates included a first installment of £25,000 for a new school and three years later the Governor planted a fig tree on the Kileleshwa site. Although building had started in 1947 it was not completed until 1952 and parents could at last be assured their daughters would enjoy "highest civilized conditions." Each house of fifty girls would have its own housemistress, two assistant mistresses (single women teachers), a matron, and servants. There would be no need to send a daughter "home" to Britain for her secon-

---

[1] *East African Standard* (Nairobi), January 30, 1946.

dary education for here was a school in the colony that could give her academic, moral, and social training comparable to the English public schools. She would, in fact, probably be better cared for and even more comfortable than under the Spartan conditions of many English schools. Furthermore, graduate teachers recruited from Britain would prepare her for the Cambridge examinations. In the halycon days of postwar prosperity the European community were growing ever more confident that Kenya was indeed white man's country, and it was only proper to educate their sons at the Prince of Wales and Duke of York schools and their daughters at Kenya High —all in the best traditions of English education. No African or Asian children were admitted because the three races had their separate schools, a system that everyone assumed would continue indefinitely. Only in his wildest dreams, if then, did a European believe that Africans would win their independence in a decade.

If Kenya High School is a monument to the European's feeling of permanence, it is also a memorial to an illustrious principal. Miss J. M. A. Stott came to Kenya High in 1942 and it was her single-minded passion, great energy, and persuasive power over the Ministry of Education that in good part accounts for the growth of the school. During her twenty-one years as principal she opened the Sixth Form and began sending her girls to British universities; she worked with horticulturists in landscaping the new campus, and after the official opening of the new buildings she led campaigns for a swimming pool and chapel. Just prior to her departure, in 1963, she laid the foundation stone of a new library. But she did more than raise buildings; she established a well-ordered community in which girls could work without outside distraction and over which parents need have no concern for their daughters' care. Academic standards were set high and it was a rare event in later years if more than one or two girls among 120 failed to win a School Certificate. Sixth Formers were prepared for honour rather than pass degrees in British universities and it was with great pride that the principal announced on Speech Day in 1961 that the first Cambridge scholarship to be won by any boy or girl in Kenya had come to Kenya High. The award was offered by Newnham College in Physics, and Miss Stott regarded it as "the highest honour in the scholastic world."

By 1961 Janette Stott knew that change was coming. In January of that year she admitted two African and four Asian students, the first European school head to do so. Both an acceptance of change and a belief in tradition are evident in her final two Speech Day reports:

> As you go down the drive this evening look back will you at the Chapel which you as parents built. It stands compact, solid, very peaceful against the evening sky. It is significant that you built this at a time which stood on the threshold of great change though you may not have known it. It stands now at the centre of the school as a symbol of unchanging faith, hope and love which God has given to human beings to be rediscovered by the young.[2]

When she announced her retirement in 1962 the winds of change were blowing even harder. In her last official words to the girls and their parents she spoke less of change and more of the tradition on which the school was built:

> Remember that you belong to a great tradition; not only to the small tributary of tradition which goes back through this School, but to the great traditions of the countries of your fathers and mothers; and particularly to the English tradition of whose qualities a great Eastern writer has said, "Never since the days of the Greeks was there such a sweet, such a just, such a boyish master as the English." You are the daughters of that tradition and it should be safe in your hands.[3]

In the years to come there would be parents at Speech Day exercises who would harbour rather less tolerant views of the English tradition.

---

[2] *Principal's Report*, 1961 (in the files of the school).
[3] *Principal's Report*, 1962.

## Standards and Service

ALTHOUGH, as we shall see, Independence has brought many changes, the basic traditions of the school have continued to flourish. The next Principal, Adrienne Leevers, maintained high academic standards, gave responsibility and authority to her Sixth Formers, and placed great emphasis on accepting the obligation of service. The scholarly qualifications of the staff have also been maintained but a high proportion of teachers are now on two-year contracts, and turnover has been rapid. A group of teachers with ten or more years of experience left in 1963 when the European community had major doubts about the future stability of Kenya. Over 85 per cent of the present teaching staff are graduates and almost half of these are recruited from Britain through the Ministry of Overseas Development. Other expatriates, whether permanent residents or temporary visitors in Kenya, are recruited locally. The Principal, with the cooperation of the Ministry of Education, has retained a good deal of autonomy in making staff appointments, and through the high reputation of the school, advertisements in the British press, the Old Girls network, and local grapevines the number of applicants has remained comfortably above the list of vacancies. Under an energetic and dedicated staff new methods of teaching French and mathematics are in use and syllabus changes are taking shape in English and history. Extra duties in games and school societies are usually taken on willingly. Under Adrienne Leevers' leadership the staff developed a no-nonsense, unsentimental determination to make integration work.

Both the size (the staff student ratio is 1:13) and the diversity of the staff have allowed the school to offer a wide range of subjects. The girls in Forms I and II take all of the following subjects:

English               Art
History               Needlework
Geography             Music
French                Physical education
Mathematics           Religious education
Science               Latin or Swahili

Some subjects are, of course, given more periods each week than others. In Form II general science gives way to separate courses in biology, chemistry, and physics. Thus girls carry a dozen subjects and are almost fully occupied in all eight of the 40-minute periods each day.

In Forms III and IV a girl is guided, on the basis of her inclination and performance, into an arts, science, or general stream. It is in Form III that the subjects in which a girl will try her School Certificate examinations are decided and typical selections are as follows:

| Arts | Science | General |
| --- | --- | --- |
| English | English | English |
| Geography | History | Geography |
| History | German | Cookery |
| French | French | Art |
| Latin | Mathematics | Biology |
| Mathematics | Physics | Swahili |
| Biology | Chemistry | Mathematics |
| Art | Biology | |

Syllabuses in all subjects in Form IV, and to some extent in Form III, are determined by the Cambridge examinations, but in Forms I and II the school has a good deal of autonomy. Thus the English Department has divided the five Forms I into sets on the basis of tests given during the first term and is experimenting with various approaches to both language and literature. The staff was asked by the head of the department "to make sure by means of conversation, simple oral questions and discussion that the pupils understand spoken language." Some of the girls, the directive continued, "are not used to hearing standard English and often have difficulty at first in following what is being said to them. It is best to speak rather more slowly and clearly than usual with a longer pause between sentences." In literature the emphasis is on extensive reading rather than detailed study. The top sets may be reading *Midsummer Night's Dream* or the *Odyssey* while the lower sets are struggling through a simplified edition of *David Copperfield* and a series of readers with controlled vocabularies. The school recognizes that an African girl from a rural primary school brings to Kenya High a linguistic and literary background far different from that of a girl who has grown up in a European family and attended a European primary school. Only through an intensive study of English in Form I can the African girl begin to bridge the gap. By Form IV she will write two School Certificate papers in English language which will test comprehension, knowledge of English usage, and her capacity to compose a short essay.

The School Certificate examination in literature changed its title in 1968 from English Literature to Literature in English. The change is significant because it allows for new options including *Things Fall Apart* by the Nigerian writer Chinua Achebe, and *The Pearl* by John Steinbeck. These two, together with Shaw's *Caesar and Cleopatra* and a collection of twentieth-century narrative poems will occupy Form IV for most of the year. Again significantly, the traditional Shakespeare play now becomes optional. But the required level of School Certificate performance will remain the same and fourth formers can expect questions which may not ask them to reveal literary insight but will assume they know the content of the works read. Typical questions are these:

> *Caesar and Cleopatra:* By close reference to at least two episodes in the play, illustrate Caesar's ability to take decisive action at moments of crisis. (1966)

> *Twentieth Century Narrative Poems:* Give a brief account of two poems dealing with the supernatural which particularly

impressed you and, referring closely to the text, explain their appeal to you. (1966)

*As You Like It:* Referring closely to appropriate episodes in the play, and to actual speeches, show how Shakespeare contrasts life in the country with life at Court. (1965)

The history department has also been revising its syllabus for Forms I and II and has developed a survey course which concentrates on the ancient world in the first year and ranges over the modern world in the second. In the latter there is an opportunity to discuss Kenya's membership in the Commonwealth, her commitments to the United Nations and the Organization for African Unity, and her economic development in the fields of agriculture, industry, and transport. In the new School Certificate courses which bridge Forms III and IV the emphasis on Africa is pronounced. Form III divides its time between European (including British) history 1789–1878, and the histories of South, North, and Northeast Africa. All the time in Form IV is given over to a new syllabus on the history of East Africa from circa 1000 to the present.

The quality of teaching in Forms I to IV varies tremendously from the leadership of intelligent discussion made lively through probing and imaginative questions, to the "coverage" of a poem made tiresome by a series of what-am-I-thinking-of questions. The teaching load is twenty-eight or twenty-nine periods a week, but it is not unknown for a teacher to meet several forms and thus be required to teach four, occasionally five, different courses. Classes are never larger than thirty, and discipline is seldom a problem. At the beginning of each class the teacher is met by a monitor who greets her, offers to carry her books, and leads her to the classroom. The class stands as she enters and says, "Good morning." At the end of the period the class stands again as the teacher leaves the room. If anything, the girls are too receptive; almost docile, and their desire to do well on examinations leads many of the staff to tell instead of teach.

The school appears to be a remarkably well-ordered community with authority delegated to staff and prefects according to a time-tested set of regulations and procedures. Both the academic and the social tone of the school are in good part set by the 100 or more girls of the Sixth Form. A major strength of the school lies in its wide range of sixth-form subjects with a staff qualified to handle the scholarly demands of sixth-form teaching. Sixteen subjects in all are taught, including eight sciences. A girl normally takes three subjects at principal level over the two years of the Sixth and, as this experience is regarded as a bridge to the university, she is expected to do a good deal of independent work. The Cambridge Higher School Certificate examinations at the end of the Upper Sixth demand both breadth and depth. Candidates in history, for example, write three two-and-a-half-hour papers—*English History 1485–1714*, *European History 1494–1939*, and *World Affairs since 1939*. The European paper in 1965 included such questions as these:

> Did Napoleon I fulfill or destroy the work of the French Revolution?

and

> Consider the importance of economic factors as motives for colonial expansion in the Nineteenth century.

In 1966, twenty-one of the twenty-eight girls who wrote the examinations were awarded Higher School Certificates.

## A Secure Society

BETWEEN the end of afternoon classes and bedtime girls are in prep or games or clubs according to a carefully regulated schedule. Of the fifteen or more clubs and societies and activities the Young Farmers, the school choirs, and Scottish dancing are probably the most vigorous and popular. A girl participates in games twice a week, once in a team sport such as field hockey or swimming, and once in activities which range from judo to ping-pong. If she is a junior (Forms I and II) she is in bed and lights are out by 8:45; 9:00 for seniors; 10:15 for the Sixth Form. The regulations governing the lives of boarders must be seen not only as a part of the public school tradition but as a response to the concern of parents for maximum security for their daughters. Every girl submits to her housemistress a list, signed by her parents, of approved visitors with whom she may go out on Exeats (leave Sundays). She also submits a list of those to whom she may write. A Sixth Former, however, may have a general permission from her parents to write to whom she pleases. Each weekday the routine for supper is the same.

6:50  Bell for girls to go downstairs
6:55  Girls line up in silence
7:00  Girls walk up to supper in silent single file
7:30  Girls going to prep or clubs do not leave the dining hall until they report to staff on duty. Those returning to the House go down in pairs. They may talk but must not scream or run.

The Sixth Form have, relatively, more freedom. A member of the Upper Sixth may go out every Sunday and on several week-ends, but she may not leave the school with men or boys unless they are members of her family.

## *The Strains of Integration*

As mentioned above, both the academic standards and social conventions of the school were designed primarily for a particular clientele: English families who knew and respected the public school tradition. In recent years an increasing number of African and Asian girls have entered the school and in 1967 one-quarter of the student body was African. The proportion will, of course, increase in the immediate future as it is now

## A *Former European School: Kenya High* / 97

Ministry of Education policy to allocate to Africans one-half the Form I places in all former European schools. The implications for Kenya High of a policy of integration are worth examining.

For the 150 Form I openings in 1967 the school received only 400 applications. To fill the African quota, which in turn was broken down into provincial quotas, and maintain the normal academic standards proved to be difficult. The number of applicants was relatively small, probably because of the high level of fees. Few African families can afford £165 for tuition, boarding, and extras, plus £40 for uniforms. Government bursaries are available, but fewer than one-half of the African girls in the school are currently receiving them. The substantial fees appear to deter African girls from applying, particularly when the fees at African schools are only one-seventh as much. The result is that the African girls now being admitted to Kenya High are not academically equal to the Asian and European entry.

The dilemma is genuine because the fee structure is necessary to maintain the fabric and the traditions of the school. Both the buildings and the grounds need to be maintained and, although the subordinate staff has been reduced, it still numbers over 100. The European diet has been reduced to 3/ per girl per day but this is twice the cost of food at African schools. Houses that were designed for fifty now house fifty-six and no further expansion can be tolerated. The positions of housemistress and matron have been combined and the five servants who in an earlier day looked after 100 girls are now reduced to two. The administrative officers of the school are convinced that economies have gone about as far as they can go, and if the school is to continue to maintain its standards it will either have to keep its present fees or be financed on a different basis. (The school now relies on fees for 60 per cent of its income and on Government grants for the remainder.) On the other hand, if its policy of integration is to be successful it would appear necessary to develop a larger pool of more able

African applicants, and that presumably can be done only by reducing fees or by increasing the number of bursaries. African girls now come from a wide range of social and economic backgrounds. Their parents are employed in more than fifty different occupations but the largest group by a wide margin are the daughters of farmers. It is of course on these families that the burden of fees weighs most heavily.

The pace of integration has been swift as the table below reveals.

*Enrollment by Forms 1965–1967*

|  | 1965 Africans | 1965 Non-Africans | 1966 Africans | 1966 Non-Africans | 1967 Africans | 1967 Non-Africans |
|---|---|---|---|---|---|---|
| Form I | 50 | 126 | 44 | 97 | 53 | 88 |
| Form II | 12 | 114 | 47 | 119 | 45 | 94 |
| Form III | 4 | 103 | 8 | 95 | 43 | 107 |
| Form IV | 5 | 101 | 5 | 97 | 8 | 85 |
| Form V | 3 | 19 | 7 | 46 | 12 | 55 |
| Form VI | 4 | 45 | 3 | 28 | 7 | 34 |
| Total | 78 | 508 | 114 | 482 | 168 | 463 |

Over the two-year period the total number of African students doubled, but because of admission and selection problems discussed above African girls represented less than 40 per cent of Form I entry in 1967.

Integration has been fully achieved in the Board of Governors. The first African joined the Board in 1964. The chairman is now the Hon. Charles Njonjo, M.P., Attorney General of Kenya, and the Board is made up of five other Africans, three Europeans, and one Asian. The school has had little success in attracting Kenya citizens, particularly Africans, to its teaching staff. Kenya has produced few African women graduates and too many interesting opportunities are open to them in positions other than teaching. Kenya High appointed the first African to its teaching staff in 1963. In 1967 only five in a staff of fifty-three were Kenya citizens and only two of those were Africans.

In a new country the development of a sense of nationhood is one of the primary functions of its schools. The cultivation of a respect for tribal custom and tradition yet the need for modification of tribal rivalry, an understanding of the history of the country, and an appreciation of the role citizens can play in its development are among the several themes that give substance to the role of the school in nation building. But expatriate teachers, particularly those on two-year contracts, cannot participate in this phase of the school task with either knowledge or conviction. Nor at the moment can the majority of Kenya High pupils. In 1967 only 40 per cent of its girls were Kenya citizens, and whether the others, daughters of European and Asian families, will remain in Kenya throughout their adult lives is impossible to predict.

In this respect the school is a microcosm of the uncertainties and anxieties of independent Kenya. Whether the country will emerge as a genuinely integrated, multiracial society or an African society in which the immigrant races are tolerated is a question that applies equally to the school. Meanwhile, the strains and tensions that go with achieving integration are keenly felt. A segment of the European girls come from families that have taken white superiority for granted and they carry with them to school the prejudices of their parents. Asian girls reflect the very considerable uncertainty of their community in the future development of Kenya and tend to retreat into docility. The African girls come from very different backgrounds—from the homes of cabinet ministers to the thatched huts of peasant farmers. Before coming to the school some of the girls were not accustomed to using knives and forks or sleeping between sheets, while others had grown up in Nairobi in a thoroughly urban style of life. The girls come not only from different racial and economic backgrounds but represent over twenty nationalities (Nairobi has an increasing diplomatic corps and an international business community) and half a dozen religions. With such a diversity of students it will take time for the school to develop a common purpose and a sense of unity. It can no longer take for granted the similarities of outlook, attitudes, and values which girls formerly brought with them almost as a part of their uniform. Nor can the school take for granted that all its cherished traditions will be accepted by new students. African girls of sixteen or seventeen in Form I are reluctant to accept their status as "rabble" (the school term for juniors) and show proper respect for Form IV European girls who may be younger. And Europeans are not accustomed to accepting the authority of Asian or African prefects.

If neither the theme of nation building nor a common religious faith can give the school a sense of direction and purpose, on what basis of unity can it build? Diversity is itself an asset not a liability, and the creation of a school society with girls from a multiplicity of races, nationalities, religions, and income levels, who can tolerate difference and search for common values, is now felt to be a unifying theme. And this means that the windows of the school will face not only East Africa or Britain but a large segment of the world as girls increasingly go to live and work in many nations. But in this new context of diversity the school staff believe that the older traditions will still be needed. Behind the emphasis on academic standards lies a high regard for scholarship and a belief in the intrinsic value of the liberal arts and sciences. These values may need to be transmitted to students of an emerging society that tends to regard the winning of a School Certificate as the goal of a secondary education. The development of ethical standards, and the capacity to accept responsibility and wield authority are similarly deep within the public school tradition and regarded by the school as no less important in a multiracial and diverse community.

Janette Stott recognized the adaptability of tradition as

she reflected on it during one of her last Speech Day reports. Her remarks are prophetic:

> Many of you here today were once girls in the school. Some of you will remember it as you found it in buildings which you shared with the Nairobi Primary School so that you could not even call your school your own. You lived in wooden huts where open fires heated your bath water, where you did prep and had your free time in dormitories because there were no common rooms. . . . Yet the tradition of today was planted there and flourished in spite of its difficulties. The school you look at today may appear very different but in spirit it is the same as the school you helped found. . . .
>
> Purpose is given us to take all that is best in human nature and increase it until goodness flows out from the young in this school of all races beyond the walls of a school into the country and the world of the next generation.[4]

Before that prophecy can be fulfilled there are, as we have seen, one or two problems that demand attention. The pace of integration may need to be reduced in order to give present students a little time to learn and live with each other in harmony and thus set a tone and climate for new arrivals. A decision should be made on the school's finances; whether in future years it should expect to derive a major share of its income from fees or from government grants. If the present fee structure is maintained, the difficulty of enrolling seventy-five able African girls a year (half the Form I entry) must be faced and the need made clear for more generous bursaries. Similarly, the school and the Ministry of Education should reach a compromise agreement on economy measures which can be enforced. These will, in turn, depend on the fee structure that is maintained. Probably no solution can be found to the problem of staff turnover in a period when the majority of teachers will be expatriates on short-term contracts. There is a pressing concern, however, to recruit African and Asian staff, either those

---

[4] *Principal's Report*, 1961.

who will shortly be trained at University College, Nairobi, or graduates returning from universities overseas.

Meanwhile, the school is becoming an integrated society and its intentions are expressed in one of the verses of the new version of the school song.

> Gathered here from many races, one in purpose all shall be;
> Banished fear, forgotten hatred, till we reign in liberty,
> And with wonder men discover faith in world-wide brotherhood,
> *Servire est regnare, servire est regnare.*

[CHAPTER SEVEN]

## An African School: Alliance

### Strong to Serve

ALLIANCE HIGH SCHOOL is a national institution and the cradle of African leadership in Kenya. Eight years before Independence two of its Old Boys were the first Africans to serve as Minister and Parliamentary Secretary; in the first year of Independence more than half the Cabinet and three-fourths of the Permanent Secretaries in the new African Government had attended Alliance. Since its founding in 1926 it has enrolled the cream of primary school leavers and it now has boys from thirty-seven tribes. When 15,000 candidates recently applied for the ninety places in Form I the Ministry of Education had to invent screening devices the following year to cut applications in half. When Alliance's second Headmaster died in 1966 Kenya's House of Representatives stood silent in his memory and President Kenyatta recorded his appreciation of "the great work that Carey Francis, one of the greatest educationalists that Kenya ever had, did for this country and her people."

Carey Francis, a strong and colorful personality, was Head for twenty-two years. He brought with him to Kenya many of the traditions of the English public school but none more significant than the influence of the Headmaster. When he retired it could be said that Alliance was Carey Francis writ large. His insistance on obedience, punctuality, and cheerfulness, his belief that every boy should play games and keep fit, and his encouragement of a score of activities and societies were only a part of his legacy. The "terrifying earnestness" as he once described the motivation of young Africans was given order and direction, and year after year every boy in Form IV won a School Certificate. But behind the emphasis on scholarship, and the development of character through games, and the training in leadership offered to prefects, there lay a central core of Christian faith. It was, indeed it still is, a faith that stresses service rather than reflection; and it gave to the school its basic purpose which Headmaster Francis formulated in the school motto, Strong to Serve, and in the school prayer:

> Have in Thy keeping, O Lord Our God this school; that its work may be thorough and its life joyful, that from it may go out, strong in body and mind and character, men who in Thy Name and with Thy power, will serve their fellows faithfully.

The school occupies 150 acres of valley, ridge, and woodland in the midst of small Kikuyu farms. Staff houses are far enough from classrooms for teachers to drive to work. School buildings, all of one story with a cut-stone exterior, are severe in their simplicity and modestly equipped. The only variety is achieved by the chapel with its suggestion of an Old Testament tabernacle, and the Hall, a two-story stone hexagonal. The chapel, which can seat 500 boys, was completed in 1966 for £9,500, and a dormitory for thirty-two boys equipped with beds, lockers, and a washing and sanitation unit cost only £4,000. Staff houses are comfortable but not luxurious. Each teacher, married or single, has his own house and employs at least one servant or possibly two. English-style hedges enclose well-manicured lawns and flower beds and screen servants' quarters at the rear. At an altitude of 6,700 feet it is never hot and for several months of the year the staff light their fireplaces each evening. Mornings in July and August are damp and cold but for most of the year the days are sunny and fluffs of white cumulus build up over the Kikuyu *shambas* of maize, beans, and coffee.

## A Complex Society

THE school day at Alliance starts early and by 7:15 the boys are not only up and dressed but have made their beds and cleaned and tidied their dormitories. Close by the entrance to the chapel they assemble in quasi-military formation by houses for morning call-over and announcements. A chapel service of one hymn, short talk, and prayer follows, and the boys and their masters go off to breakfast. Eight periods of forty minutes each constitute the school day and only the Sixth Formers could be said to have any free periods. The late afternoons are given over to games or the meetings of school societies, and a visitor walking through the compound would find boys practising football and track; a meeting of Scouts, the Science Society, and the choir; boys studying in their form rooms or reading in the crowded library; and a master and his wife teaching fifty boys the elements of country dancing. In an earlier day when the missionary influence was strong this was the only dancing permitted, but even now when other dances, tribal and modern, are sanctioned the boys continue to like the country dance of Scotland. An hour-and-a-half of prep follows dinner and at 8:30 at the end of a busy day a boy in the main school (Forms I–IV) has an hour to himself before bedtime.

This school is, clearly, a highly structured and complex society. In addition to the academic schedule, there are some twenty-five clubs or societies, a program of games which changes each term, chapel services morning and (voluntarily) in the evening, and occasional major events such as Field Day or the production of a Shakespeare play. All these require delegation of authority by the Head to masters and prefects, and a willing acceptance of responsibility by the boys themselves. Evening prep is a good example. A few minutes only after the bell all boys are at work in their form rooms without benefit of supervision. A duty prefect may walk occasionally past the windows, but it is boys themselves who set the no-nonsense tone of evening study. That every boy will participate in games is as deeply rooted a belief at Alliance as it is in an English public school. Whether it is for fun, or to keep fit, for the honor and glory of his house and school, or because he is obliged to play, every boy chooses a sport in the first and third terms and competes in athletics (track and field events) in the second. Under the coaching and supervision of masters and prefects the standards of performance are high, particularly in football and athletics. It is not unusual for first and second football elevens to go unbeaten throughout the season and for athletics teams to place first in all-Kenya meets. This competitive drive is not new. An entry in the school diary for 1926 runs, "The AHS football team because of the lack of transport *walked* to Nairobi [fifteen miles], played in the Police Shield Final and won, and walked back again."

For the boys and young men of Alliance living arrangements are simple and austere. Breakfast is bread, jam, and tea; lunch is a vegetable stew, and dinner is a meat stew, with rice or dumplings twice a week. Fruit is added twice a week, and on Sundays each boy has a hard-boiled egg. This menu was set in 1964 and it has continued week after week ever since simply because it is the best diet that the school can provide for 1/50, the maximum grant allowed per boy per day.

Residence life too has its austerities. Sixteen boys sleep in one section of a dormitory on double-decker bunks. Each boy has a locker but no desk or other equipment. He takes showers and washes his clothes (including his sheets) in cold water, and in rotation he is responsible for cleaning, not only his dormitory, but all the other buildings except the school hall and chapel. There is no matron to look after his clothes, and no nurse to look after his ailments. He does this himself or with the help of prefects.

## A Climate for Learning

THE absence of amenities does not deter boys from applying for admission to Alliance. Each December the Head and his staff cut mounds of applications down to 1,000 on the basis of character reference and rank in class as reported by primary school headmasters. Usually only the first three boys from a school are considered. A team of ten staff members then administer short arithmetic and English comprehension tests and conduct interviews both on campus and in the provinces. Interviews may sometimes last only two or three minutes but they serve to give the staff a general impression of a boy. The interviews and tests reduce the applications to 600 and the vital factor in selection then becomes the Kenya Preliminary Examination. Boys are chosen from all provinces and most of the counties in Kenya.

The school year begins in January and is divided into three terms with vacations in April, August, and December-January. In Forms I and II a boy takes thirteen subjects over a forty-period week.

| | |
|---|---|
| English | 8 |
| Mathematics | 6 |
| History | 3 |
| Geography | 3 |
| Chemistry | 3 |
| Physics | 2 |
| Biology | 3 |
| French (form II only) | 2 |
| Art and woodwork | 2 |
| Religious knowledge | 2 |
| Physical education | 1 |
| Music | 1 |
| Swahili | 1 |

In Form III a boy is obliged to make a decision, under guidance from the staff, on the choice of his School Certificate subjects. All boys write eight papers, some nine, from the list below:

| | |
|---|---|
| English language | Biology |
| Literature in English | Physics with chemistry or |
| History | Physics and chemistry |
| Geography | Swahili or French or |
| Mathematics | Religious knowledge |

The choices are limited and the curriculum is patterned on English secondary grammar schools of an earlier day. If given the facilities and the teachers, Alliance would be only too willing to carry a boy to School Certificate level in art, music, crafts, and agriculture. Boys can, however, work in these fields outside the curriculum; school choirs and a Young Farmers Club, for example, are flourishing. A belief long held in England appears to have taken root at Alliance that it is possible to learn something without taking a course in it.

Very considerable stress is placed on English, and eight periods a week are divided between language and literature in each of the four years. In the lower forms the emphasis is on extensive reading and each class is provided with a class library of more than fifty titles including such authors as Dickens, Stevenson, Conan Doyle, and Jules Verne. A good deal of writing is assigned and at least five minutes of every English lesson are given over to improving spoken English through drills on stress, intonation, and rhythm. Extensive reading continues in Form III but more attention is given to books of School Certificate standard, particularly those prescribed in previous years. In Form IV the boys get a lot of practice in writing the kinds of essays they will meet in both the language and literature School Certificate papers. Five books chosen from a broad list constitute the syllabus in literature and Alliance chose the following in 1968:

Bernard Shaw: *Caesar and Cleopatra*
Chinua Achebe: *Things Fall Apart*

William Shakespeare: *Macbeth*
Nevil Shute: *No Highway*
Arthur Grimble: *A Pattern of Islands*

There is probably less cramming at Alliance than at most schools because the boys have confidence in their teachers and will accept a modification of the prescribed courses. But anxieties build up and Form IV boys usually ask not to be taught but to be allowed to study in the final month; and it is not uncommon to find a boy in bed long after lights out reading or memorizing his notes by flashlight. This is the "terrifying earnestness" to which Carey Francis referred and it makes teaching at Alliance at once both a joy and a trial. Discipline problems are almost unknown and boys are cooperative, eager, and receptive. But their eagerness usually does not stem from a love of learning and an interest in a subject but out of a concern to get a good "School Cert." Teachers are therefore tempted to give model answers and to coach carefully. One boy reflected this in admiring a member of the staff; "He's a very good teacher; he gives us good notes." It is of course possible for teachers to range out and beyond the School Certificate syllabus and still achieve good results; indeed the results are probably better because of the excursions. But these are the more experienced teachers whose pupils over the years have done well. They now have the confidence of the boys and can teach flexibly. The school officially discourages cramming but recognizes the importance of examinations in the lives of its boys and is, in fact, proud of its record. Over a period of twenty-seven years only twelve in a total of 960 have failed to win a School Certificate.

The introduction of new syllabuses, particularly those now emerging in mathematics and science with an emphasis on principles and concepts rather than computation and facts, will help to break the power that examinations now hold over the secondary schools. Under these syllabuses it will not be possible to coach students for a predictable series of questions. Both the senior mathematics and chemistry masters at Alliance are working with teachers in other schools and, with the blessing of the Cambridge Examinations Syndicate, are preparing new syllabuses and the texts to go with them. With the assistance of the School Mathematics Project (the English fountainhead of the new mathematics) a group of math teachers in Kenya have produced a new series of texts for Forms I–IV. After adequate trial runs these will become the basis for a new School Certificate mathematics syllabus. The school would like to adopt Nuffield chemistry but the cost of equipment is beyond the scope of the Chemistry Department's budget. Under present stringencies the Department is allocated only £130 per year or 7/ per student.

### Headmaster and Staff

ON one occasion Carey Francis exclaimed, "I wonder whether there is any other school in the world with such a staff—each giving himself, seeking how much he can do with no word of unpleasantness or grumble for years past." They do indeed work hard, teaching thirty periods each week, coaching and refereeing games, assisting the societies, and assuming all manner of duties related to the health, cleanliness, and physical upkeep of the school. Some of the staff are housemasters, others take responsibility for the library, the bookstore, chapel services, and the school magazine. The school employs cooks and a few workmen, but no matron or cateress, and certainly few administrative staff. Thus the school is operated essentially by the Headmaster, a bursar and accountant, the teaching staff, and the boys.

The recruitment and selection of a staff both willing and able to accept such a range of responsibility falls to the Headmaster. He works closely with the Ministry of Overseas Development of the British Government, and on occasion has flown to London to interview candidates. He would, of course, prefer to employ an increasing number of African graduates, but they are in short supply and usually after a few terms at Alliance are whisked off by the Ministry of Education to become headmasters elsewhere. In 1967 only one African graduate was on the Alliance staff; there were two nongraduate African teachers and twenty-one expatriates—all British.

Normally there are three expatriate applications for every two posts and only those with high qualifications are advised to apply. An honours degree, two or more years of experience, and good references are the basic requirements, but the Headmaster probes more deeply hoping to find a Christian commitment, a willingness to become a member of the school community, and skills and experience that will be valuable outside the classroom. The expatriate staff are well paid and well housed. Staff houses on the other side of campus from the boys' dormitories carry a subsidized rent of 140/ per month and have two or three bedrooms, indoor sanitation, hot water, and electricity. Staff salaries, paid by the Kenya Government, are topped off generously by the British Government. These salaries together with ample leaves, education allowances for children, paid passages, and other benefits make expatriate teaching no financial hardship. And frequently a two- or four-year stay at Alliance gives a young teacher such a range of experience and responsibility that he can return to Britain and qualify for a position well up in a school hierarchy.

There is relatively little teaching that could be described as imaginative or innovative, probably because the majority of the staff are too busy with other activities to give adequate time to planning courses and preparing daily lessons. But the school could not operate if the staff were only classroom teachers. The Alliance traditions places high value on maintaining the social and spiritual life of the school at a high level. The staff are thus involved in far more than the intellectual development of their boys. Directing a play or preparing a chapel talk or refereeing a match is an intrinsic part of the teacher's job although it may mean that tomorrow's classes will be little more than a coverage of the text.

Behind all the staff's many activities lies a deep commitment, much of which the Headmaster has helped to create:

> The staff of Alliance *care* about what happens to the school, to the boys, to education in Kenya. With their wives and families they give greatly of their time and talents in all ways and in supporting me and the Board. It's a great thing in a school when both the Headmaster and the students know that the staff care.[1]

When Laurence Campbell became Headmaster in 1963 he knew Alliance from the inside. He had taught English and history from 1952 to 1956 and had then left to train teachers and supervise mission schools. When he was appointed to the headship he knew much about African culture and could speak both Swahili and Kikuyu, he recognized the great contribution made by the mission societies but knew there were blemishes on the record, and he was an educator dedicated to keeping the Christian faith at the centre of the Alliance tradition:

> From the first Alliance has set out to be a Christian family of boys and masters. The heart of everything is our primary loyalty to Jesus Christ. This does not just mean that we have Chapel services and R.K. lessons and other 'pious' activities, though these exist and are important. It means that all we do—class work, games, school life, personal relationships, as well as Chapel and the rest—should be seen as service we offer to our Master. Through all these we seek to serve Him and to help our boys to become strong, intelligent, Christian men.[2]

Furthermore, his scholarly credentials were impeccable (MA, Edinburgh), he was an enthusiastic athlete and a certified track coach, and he was blessed with an intelligent and charming wife.

There can be little doubt that he has put his imprint on the school. Partly by exhortation but mainly by example he stretches his staff. He occasionally runs with the cross country

---

[1] *Headmaster's Report*, 1966 (in the files of the school).

[2] *Headmaster's Notes to New Members of Staff* (in the files of the school).

team, gives talks on current affairs, has directed Shakespeare plays, and regularly teaches seventeen periods a week. Under this example willing staff are encouraged, in his words, "to find where their limits are." He also believes he must, as a moral and spiritual leader, articulate to his boys what he expects of them.

Thus he has weekly talks with Form IV on such topics as careers or boy-girl relationships and with the Sixth Form on controversial political issues. On Saturday morning he speaks to the whole school on some aspect of world affairs. "If I am to be effective," he says, "they've got to know me and I to know them." His teaching schedule (English and religious knowledge) is so arranged that he has taught all boys in the school before they reach Form IV. And he is confident that he knows the name of every boy in the school. Present enrollment is 460. The Headmaster of Alliance is, as we have seen, expected to be a national leader, and L. J. Campbell is no exception. As a member of the Council of the University of East Africa, the Vice-Chairman of the Christian Churches' Education Association, and as Chairman of the Headmaster's Association for three years he has served Kenya well. It would of course be impossible to play these many roles without a capacity to delegate responsibility to both staff and prefects. Indeed one of his strengths as Head in his close relationship with his prefects.

## Prefects and the Sixth Form

A FORMER member of the British Cabinet once remarked that of the various responsibilities he had held in his life the one that he took most seriously was his prefectship at Winchester. An Alliance prefect might say the same. As leaders who keep the school disciplined and punctual in its day-to-day operation, who supervise the dormitories and control the dining hall, the prefects do much to set the school tone. There are forty-eight prefects, all in the Sixth Form, chosen by the Head after consultation with his staff. Each Friday morning the nine senior prefects meet to review the past week. Two of them are in charge of food and the kitchen, another with a staff of assistants (all trained in first aid) looks after matters of health, and a third with ten helpers keeps the library classified and catalogued. At the top of the prefect hierarchy are the school captain and deputy captain who serve as a bridge between the other prefects and the Headmaster. Young and inexperienced members of staff have been known to complain that the school captain wields far more authority than they.

When the Sixth Form opened in 1961 Carey Francis reported to his Speech Day audience, "The change is a major one. That it is right I have no doubt: on the one side the work belongs to, and is better done by, a school than a university; on the other the school needs a Sixth Form to head it up." As we have seen, the prefects do indeed head it up but at the same time, and, incredibly, they meet the scholarly demands of the Sixth. Boys normally take three principal subjects on either the arts or science side and one subsidiary subject over a two-year period. In some subjects, English for example, three examination papers are required; one on prose and poetry, a second on drama, and a third on a group of novels and short stories. In recent years Alliance has emphasized science in the Sixth Form largely because of Kenya's manpower needs. This has meant overcrowding the laboratories by admitting twenty-eight in labs designed for eighteen and overworking the science department staff, but the results were fully up to Alliance standards. In 1967, every "boy" in Sixth Form qualified for university entrance.

Almost all Sixth Formers are in their early twenties (the average age of boys entering Form I is 16.5), and their maturity is revealed not only in their leadership of the school but in the range of their information and the quality of questions they are raising on political and religious issues. In 1964, under the stimulation of one of the masters, the Sixth Form organized a Theological Society which now meets three times a term, invites students from other schools, and rallies an attendance of 150 or more at its meetings. Members enjoy recalling that the Society sprang from a chance remark made at a meeting of the Philosophical Society: "Of course I'm a Christian, but let's look at this thing intelligently." In recent years links have been established with Roman Catholic and Muslim leaders, several of whom have given lectures. Topics have included "Is it possible to prove the existence of God?" and "Islam and the Modern World." In these meetings boys were raising questions that had not been heard on the Alliance compound before. The Missionary Society tradition was conservative theologically, and if in years past boys dared to raise questions on, say, the Resurrection, they were referred to the authority of the Bible. But now boys are questioning that authority too and among Sixth Formers there is the beginning of a shaking of the school's foundations.

Similarly the boys are raising political and social questions with considerable sophistication. Under Carey Francis the world of affairs was pretty well kept out of the school but Laurence Campbell has opened the windows and the school will not be the same. Through his own Saturday morning talks, his invitation to political leaders and ambassadors, and his encouragement of open discussion, the Headmaster has stimulated his Sixth Form to a sharper awareness of the issues and problems that bedevil an independent and developing country. And with that awareness has arisen a concern over the growing gulf between the haves and have-nots in African society and a criticism of some of the national leaders. In a recent discussion on population control one boy remarked, "How can we expect the peasants to have small families when a Cabinet Minister has ten children?"

## A Lighthouse Role?

CHANGE has come slowly to Alliance and outwardly the school, although larger in enrollment, does not appear to have changed markedly since Independence. (Even during the height of the Emergency in 1954 with Mau Mau tensions swirling all around it the school remained calm and unruffled and all the boys won their School Certificates.) It has held its senior staff and has retained a high morale, probably because of high-quality leadership. And underneath these factors lie the underpinnings of a religious belief. Alliance has had in fact many advantages over former European schools. It has remained entirely African and thus has escaped the tensions of integration; it has admitted very few boys who are not Protestants and has continued to place great emphasis on Christian service; its boys are all bright; and it has a well-deserved reputation for developing African leadership. The school motto has had, certainly since Independence, an almost immediate relevance for its Old Boys. In a word, the school has been blessed with both a strong sense of purpose and an inner unity.

But what of the future? Will there be similar openings for today's—let alone tomorrow's—Old Boys as in the recent past? Prior to Independence the layer of educated Africans was very thin and when an African Government came to power there was room at the top for almost every Old Boy who had finished Alliance and gone on to university—room in the Cabinet, the upper reaches of the Civil Service, in university professorships, and in all phases of the public and private sector. Most of those openings have now been filled and new ones are developing rather slowly. If this analysis is correct, Alliance boys may have to reduce their career expectations, and in turn the morale of the school may suffer.

Paradoxically, one of the school's chief assets since Independence has been its near poverty. With a full knowledge of Kenya's limited resources the boys and the staff have tightened their belts and made do on an almost totally inadequate budget. Fees have remained low at 450/ per year for tuition and board. The low level of fees means, of course, that the school relies essentially on annual grants from the Ministry of Education, and in recent years these have been cut sharply. As a result, the school does not have adequate books and supplies, it cannot introduce new curriculum in science, it is understaffed administratively, and it is obliged to feed its boys on 1/50 per day with a diet containing 2,100 calories. So far morale has not suffered and the tone of the school is buoyant. But when there is not enough money for books or maps, chemicals or meals, the quality of education suffers, and the Head and his staff are too preoccupied with finances to keep their minds on teaching. The austerity budget is having another effect in preventing the school from becoming a beacon lighting the way for other schools to follow. With an able and enthusiastic staff, more expatriate continuity than most schools, and African teachers who frequently become headmasters, the school could provide a natural setting for the introduction of new subjects (agriculture in the main school, accounting in the Sixth Form, for example), pilot programs to test new syllabuses, the direct method of teaching languages, and experiments with programed learning. But these involve specialized staff and equipment neither of which are now financially possible. Instead of developing a climate of innovation Alliance is forced to remain educationally conservative.

The school recognizes the need for better facilities, and in the fall of 1967, largely on the initiative of the Headmaster, launched an international appeal to raise £150,000. These funds will be used for science development, student and staff accommodation, classroom and library expansion, and art and music rooms all with a view not only of improving present facilities, but of increasing the size of the Sixth Form and moving total enrollment towards 600. (If the development program sounds ambitious for the amount of money to be raised it should be remembered that simple design and low labor costs made it possible, at least when the campaign was launched, to build four classrooms for £6,000.) With these improved facilities and, one may hope, adequate annual grants Alliance will be in a position to maintain its leadership role.

In the years since its founding the school has had a profound effect on the life of Kenya. By far the majority of its boys have come from humble homes, the first of their family to enjoy a secondary education. Their motivation has been high but it was based on a severe practicality. As one Sixth Former has put it, "I think I see the forces that made the African learn to make a home, or fire, and the like at work today although at a higher level. The African has to learn or starve and he has to learn or be a nobody. This is why the African learns. His initiative is aroused essentially by his immediate needs." This may help to explain the "terrifying earnestness" to gain a School Certificate but it is not the kind of educational goal that Alliance has set for itself.

The school has quite consciously attempted to modify that concern for the immediate in two ways. On the one hand it has developed in its boys a sense of Christian service and has endowed their lives with the virtues of simplicity, integrity, and work cheerfully undertaken. And it has also created, at least in the Sixth Form, a genuine and lasting interest in the life of the mind and the appetite to explore political and religious questions. It has, in short, mediated the practicality of "School Cert." and has attempted to create for Kenya a responsible and dedicated élite.

[CHAPTER EIGHT]

# A Pilot School: Chavakali

## Maragoli Country

BETWEEN the two houses a cow is tethered and below the grass plot stands a grove of bananas. Beyond these is the river, full now and muddy after the long rains. Up the slope from the house hybrid maize stands 8 to 10 feet tall, and beyond it Enos' father has planted half an acre of tea. The houses are rectangular with heavily thatched roofs and clay-plastered-over-wattle walls. The parents' home is partitioned into four sections. A sitting room is furnished with two locally made wooden chairs, and in one corner a hen is brooding. In another room a vegetable stew is balanced on two stones over a wood fire. The smoke escapes under the eaves. A small storage room holds the utensils and gourds for carrying and storing water. Parents and younger children sleep in one bedroom, and each night the cow is brought into a back room of the house. The older boys occupy a smaller house divided into two bedrooms and a study. Magazine photographs, newspaper clippings, and Christmas cards cover the walls of the study, and Enos' brother who is studying for his KPE works at a sturdy wooden table. Light comes through the door and through a 12-inch window in each room. The family shares a lantern and small paraffin lamps the size of candles.

The Luhasos live on 3 acres some 12 miles from the Equator in the Western Province of Kenya. This is Maragoli country, green from 60 or more inches of rain a year, and temperate at an altitude of 5,000 feet. It is the most densely populated section of Kenya (1,500 or more per square mile) and few families own more than four acres. They grow maize and bananas, tea or coffee, but seldom both, and have a family income that will vary between £5 and £10 a year. There is usually enough food for the six or seven children in each family but malnutrition is common.

Maragoli statistics may help to explain why Enos Luhaso is at Chavakali Secondary School. There is no future at home for a boy with two brothers and a family farm of 3 acres. Through Chavakali Enos' older brother got his School Certificate and is now a clerk in one of the ministries in Nairobi. He is able to send enough money home for Chavakali fees so that Enos too may escape, and in turn Enos will no doubt help his younger brother. If three boys can get a secondary education their parents need have no worry about their old age. It is understandable that Mr. Luhaso is enthusiastic about Chavakali because, like the British or American parent who wants his son to get a "good education," he knows that schools and colleges issue certificates that open doors to a better life. From his limited income he even helped to get Chavakali started, and he may have heard of hybrid maize for the first time when his oldest son told the family about the school demonstration plots. But whatever the school may have taught his boys in new courses like agriculture and industrial arts, he believes that its main purpose is to get them a School Certificate.

### A Quaker Founding

CHAVAKALI could not have been founded without the foresight, dedication, and tolerance for frustration of a group of American Quakers. The involvement of the Society of Friends in education in Kenya goes back to 1902 when a small group of Quakers from the American Midwest took over a thousand acres of land in Western Kenya and began the Friends Africa

Industrial Mission. From the beginning, education was a major emphasis of the missionary enterprise and within Friends' education there was a strong practical emphasis. The mission prospered and in the early sixties some irreverent souls could speak of a Quaker empire of some 2,100 square miles north and east of Lake Victoria, in which Friends were managing 300 primary schools, a teacher training college, and four secondary schools. When American Quakers, soon after Independence, turned over to Africans the full administration of the mission at Kaimosi the East Africa Yearly Meeting had a membership of 30,000 Africans.

It was in this Quaker setting that Chavakali began. American Friends were conscious of the limited number of Africans who found their way into secondary schools and were dubious about the strictly academic curriculum which these schools had adopted. In 1956 Fred Reeve, the executive secretary of the mission, while on home leave, shared some of his concerns with Friends at Earlham, a Quaker college in Indiana. Earlham was interested but had neither the funds nor the staff to initiate a program of technical assistance on its own. For nearly two years discussion went on intermittently with the International Cooperation Administration of the United States Government, but it was not until Landrum Bolling, Earlham's new president, visited Kenya that the wheels began to move. A Reeve-Bolling proposal was presented to British colonial officials and tribal leaders and this in turn was sent to the Colonial Office in London and to ICA in Washington. Such were the complexities of initiating a request for technical assistance. The proposal made a case for increasing the teacher training college facilities at Kaimosi, the opening of an adult education program, and the development of a rural high school that would teach practical subjects in the Maragoli locations.

Meanwhile, back on the locations the wheels were also turning. When tribal leaders learned of the proposal to open a new secondary school they decided to express local enthusiasm in a tangible way. They rallied wide popular support for an annual tax of 12/50 to be collected from every family for a period of four years. So keen was the hunger for a new school that the people could not wait for Nairobi and London and Washington to make up their minds; with the first-year proceeds of the levy Chavakali opened in January, 1959, with thirty-five boys, two teachers, and no headmaster. It was the first day secondary school in Kenya and the first to be initially financed from local sources. But its birth was premature. For several months the proposal moved from one bureaucracy to another while the school shared facilities with a Friends' intermediate (upper primary) school. The Government of Kenya agreed to accept it as a maintained school and pay annual operating costs, and the Friends Africa Mission were willing to advance funds for new buildings. But when a year went by with no sign of staff or equipment from ICA, the Maragoli began to feel let down. Finally, in February, 1960, when the school had taken in its second entry and was barely existing with staff borrowed from the mission, a contract was signed in Washington.

Under the contract and with a grant of $310,685 Earlham College would set up a pilot project with the objective of developing a new pattern of secondary education for Kenya and tailored to meet the needs of Africans with emphasis on vocational education to prepare for careers in trades, agriculture, industry, teaching, and community leadership. Some assistance was provided for Kaimosi Training College, but at the core of the contract was Chavakali. Earlham would recruit a headmaster and teachers for agriculture and industrial arts, and furnish tractors and other farm implements, woodworking and metalworking machinery, and hand tools. Kenya would provide classrooms, shops, laboratory facilities, and staff housing. The coordinator of the project would be Lewis Hoskins, a history professor at Earlham. The original participants now agree that it was not a good contract: the objectives of the project were stated too vaguely and the attempt to link secondary education at Chavakali and primary teacher training at

Kaimosi was ill-advised. The division of financial responsibility between ICA and Kenya was not made fully clear, and there was no specific provision in the original contract for the training of African teachers. It was scheduled to run for two years but was later renewed for another sixteen months.

When Morris Kirk, the new Headmaster, and Robert Maxwell and Chester Bergey, the teachers of agriculture and industrial arts, arrived in July, 1960, it was eighteen months since the school had opened and morale was very low. Teachers of English had changed several times during the year and at the end of the second term there was a complete turnover of staff. Enrollment was now ninety and boys were beginning to ask for transfers to boarding schools or an improvement in conditions at Chavakali. Otherwise, they said, they would have little hope of passing School Certificate examinations. From the beginning, Gill House (the headquarters of the Ministry of Education) gave the project only grudging support. Colonial civil servants were reserved in their enthusiasm for a plan to transplant an American rural high school into Western Kenya. They accepted Chavakali as a maintained school, largely because of its impressive local support, but once the ICA contract was signed, there was a reluctance in Gill House to give the project full support. Within a month of his arrival as Headmaster, Morris Kirk was writing, "A major difficulty seems to be a reluctance on the part of colonial officials to honor their commitments to the experimental nature of the project and the financing of it."[1] And a year later he was convinced that the colonial administration was cutting its annual grants to Chavakali to the extent that ICA was supporting it. The result was a shortage of three classrooms, two staff houses, and one sanitation block.

In 1961 building shortages and staff turnover led to a student strike. There was no real staff stability and the Head was reduced to making staff appointments on a term-to-term basis.

---

[1] August 24, 1960.

When four teachers left at the end of Term II and only three replacements could be found, the boys felt that they should demonstrate their distress. They did not, however, enjoy good leadership and when they defied a local chief, Matthew Mwenesi, who was also chairman of the School Committee, eight boys were expelled. The incident revealed the confidence of local leadership in the school staff. Parents had been invited to visit the school and watch their boys operate the equipment and machinery which had arrived after months of delay, and the Headmaster organized a Parents Association. The School Committee found that community support was strong for the programs now beginning to flourish in agriculture and industrial arts and passed a resolution requesting the Provincial Education Office to find means of securing two African counterparts to understudy the agriculture and industrial arts teachers. In 1961 the local tax plan, the Chavakali special rate, phased out after raising £5,000 for the school over a four-year period. It was a remarkable demonstration of local support for education.

## *Agriculture and Industrial Arts*

THE foundations of the agriculture program were designed and laid by Robert Maxwell, an Iowa farmer and an experienced teacher of agriculture. On his arrival he at once entered into the life of the community, visited Maragoli farmers, and learned the ways of local agriculture. He sought the support of district officials of the Ministry of Agriculture and commercial firms that distributed agricultural machinery. Within a few months he had removed stumps and planted an acre of maize as a demonstration plot. When he had a firmer grasp of community needs his plans took shape for a school farm that would serve the dual purpose of a demonstration area for the community and a laboratory for students in agriculture courses. His objective was to teach and demonstrate to boys and their parents techniques of intensive cultivation, the use of improved varieties of maize, and the upbreeding of farm animals.

But in these early months he met opposition. The local community was more interested in establishing a secondary school than in launching an experiment. And why should the school teach agriculture? Weren't the boys attending Chavakali so that they would never need to use a *jembe* again? After watching Maxwell at work on his demonstration plot, a few parents approached the Headmaster and told him that unless the new teacher stopped working in the fields and wore better clothes they wouldn't let him teach their sons. The boys, too, were reluctant, particularly as agriculture was not a recognized School Certificate subject. But when Maxwell assured them it would become a Cambridge subject and kept referring in class to real problems and local examples that he had found as he rode his bicycle to their homes, he began to capture their interest. And when he could not put up any longer with the delay in the arrival of equipment and bought a tractor locally, trained operators, and loaned both men and machines to local farmers, the community grew more interested in the Chavakali project.

But establishing a course in the principles and practice of agriculture as a respectable subject for a secondary school was another matter. There was an existing Cambridge syllabus in agricultural science but it was not related to conditions in Kenya and it had a much more scientific than practical emphasis. The task then was to draw up a new syllabus, secure the approval of education officials in Nairobi, and submit it to the Cambridge Syndicate. Only a person of Maxwell's convictions and enthusiasm would have dared to face the problem, but he plunged into a round of letter writing and interviewing and soon became a one-man lobby for his cause. Understandably, the Ministry was cautious, and throughout most of 1961 remained dubious about whether an American team could devise and teach a syllabus that would meet Cambridge standards.

But when Maxwell won over the provincial education officer after he had visited Chavakali several times, and when the influential Minister of Agriculture, Michael Blundell, wrote a strong letter of support to Gill House, the Ministry of Education agreed to forward the syllabus to the Cambridge Syndicate. On his journey home in 1962 Maxwell stopped off in London and gathered additional support from officials in the Department of Technical Cooperation. Later the same year the Syndicate approved the syllabus, with no revisions, and Chavakali students sat for the first examination in agriculture principles and practices in November, 1963.

During Maxwell's time Chavakali was a day school and boys walked varying distances, some up to 10 miles each way every day. With seed supplied by the school they started demonstration plots on their home *shambas* and practised the crop husbandry and farm management that were now a part of the agriculture course. The results were often impressive enough to persuade parents to change over to hybrid seed and more modern methods. To supplement the course work Maxwell took his boys on field trips to well-run farms in other districts, and to agricultural exhibitions and farmers' training centres—anything that would spark their enthusiasm and change their attitudes towards farming. During vacations he arranged to have some of the boys employed by European farmers. In all these ways he made an impact on the boys and the community. Toward the end of his contract the Chavakali Parents Association wrote to the president of Earlham:

> We have observed the interest taken by students is growing steadily. . . . We hear that (Mr. Maxwell's) contract has come to an end and we are wondering whether in his case something could be done to find ways of extending his contract to bring his department in good stable state before handing over to another person. At this time when there is so much about localization, we think he will work it out so that he hands it over to a local person, who is not there now.[2]

---

[2] July 17, 1962.

Maxwell left on schedule in 1962 but came back two years later to head a USAID mission and continue on a national scale the work he had begun at Chavakali.

Industrial arts, under Chester Bergey, faced similar and even more difficult problems. Equipment was a long time in arriving from the U.S. and Bergey was forced to improvise for several months. His boys were almost totally unfamiliar with both hand tools and power equipment and they needed detailed instruction in safety measures and maintenance. Bergey gave them a good deal of training in mechanical drawing and in the use of tools before they started work on tables, bookshelves, and book boxes for their homes. He wanted to develop a course that would include instruction and practical work not only in wood, but in metal, technical drawing, and mechanics, and additional shop projects in local materials—leather, stone, and fiber. But Bergey realized the weight of tradition: "Due to the emphasis on the Cambridge School Certificate by the students and the community it was deemed necessary that we follow the Cambridge syllabus in one of these fields." [3] He chose woodworking and hoped to add other experience either as an extra or through club work. But it was a far from satisfactory arrangement because the syllabus and the examination required the boys to concentrate almost all of their time on theory and on a series of exercises in making complicated wooden joints with the use of hand tools only. With advice from specialists in related fields Bergey drew up a new and broader syllabus, and with the blessing of the Ministry of Education, sent it to the Cambridge Syndicate. It was, however, not approved and Chavakali boys have since followed the narrow woodworking syllabus.

A major weakness of the ICA-Earlham contract was the omission of any provision for counterpart training. In the summer of 1963 the contract was amended but then had only a year to run. Before Bergey left, Minoah Misaki, a P2 teacher

---

[3] Chester Bergey, *Industrial Arts Projected Work Plan for Chavakali School*, 1960 (school files).

with handicraft training, understudied him for several months and then went to an American college for a course lasting a summer and one semester. He returned to Kenya, again worked with Bergey, and took over from him on his departure. After three years Misaki returned to the United States, this time for a degree program. His departure left the school with no industrial arts teacher for two terms, and in the summer of 1968 the Headmaster was awaiting the arrival of another American. In agriculture the situation was little better. In the six years after Maxwell left, there were two Americans and two African S1 teachers of agriculture, and further changes are likely as S1's find their way into upgrading courses. Both the agricultural and industrial arts programs have suffered from too frequent a turnover of teachers, some of whom were not adequately trained. But the basic problem was a lack of foresight. Less than 1 per cent of the total funds of the AID-Earlham project was assigned to counterpart training. For several years Chavakali parents continued to look for "a local person, who is not there now."

## Chavakali in 1968

OFFICIALLY, Chavakali is still a day school, and its annual grants from the Ministry contain no assistance for boarding costs. In fact, however, it has been a boarding school since 1966 when the Maragoli again dipped into their slender resources and raised £1,200 to renovate and build two hostels. Two hundred of the total enrollment of 280 boys are now boarders who pay additional fees. The hostels are simple—starkly simple—with cement floors, tin roofs, and no ceilings; they are essentially large bare rooms filled with double- and triple-decker beds. There are no chairs, tables, or desks as the boys do all their studying in classrooms. Hostels are for sleeping and there is nothing that could be called residence life. The cost of the newer of the two hostels in terms of bed space per boy was £10.

A day starts with morning assembly in the school hall which is also the meetinghouse of the local Friends meeting. The staff, who dress informally, several in shorts and sandals, sit in a semicircle on a low platform facing the boys. A hymn led by a prefect without benefit of piano, a short talk by a member of staff, a prayer, then announcements for the day—all in fifteen minutes—and classes are ready to begin. A boy spends forty periods each week in class and long stretches of time in prep, which is supervised by prefects, not masters. Recently a group of Fourth Formers waited on the Headmaster and requested an extension of prep in the week before examinations from the normal three hours to four hours each evening. Saturday mornings and even Saturday evenings are given over to prep. Boys have little free time and may not be absent from the school compound without permission. Although the great majority are over eighteen (a few are in their late twenties and married), they accept this highly regulated life on trust: long hours with their books should produce better examination results. The worst punishment for the few who break the rules is to "walk this week," that is, revert to being a day boy and walk home each evening.

In Form I a boy takes ten subjects, including industrial arts and agriculture with double time (eight periods a week) given to English and mathematics. By the time he is in Form IV he has narrowed down to seven subjects, one of which is English, and it is on these that he writes his Cambridge examinations. There are no physical education classes above Form I and no courses in art or music. There are, however, games in the late afternoon (basketball has been successfully transplanted from America) and the Headmaster's wife, herself a recognized artist, teaches an art group that began several years ago. The concentration of time on English is needed as boys frequently enter the school never having written a paragraph or essay. In four years they must be prepared to write a composition and an English language paper, and, if they choose the English literature option, to understand such works as *The Merchant of Venice* and *Lord of the Flies*.

The routine of classes and prep is broken by clubs and school societies that meet under the care of a member of the staff. The Young Farmers Club is one of the more thriving with ninety members and a program of films, speakers, and trips. The members raise vegetables on an acre of school land and sell their produce to the school, using the profit to pay their way in the school lorry to agriculture shows and visits to settlement schemes. In all there are a dozen societies, some thriving more vigorously than others, and their health depending in good part on the enthusiasm and experience of the staff advisor.

In the past two years one of the most successful of all the activities has been the drama group. John Inglis, a teacher on sabbatical leave from Rugby, has had fifteen boys writing and producing their own plays and presenting others, such as those by Chekhov and the African dramatist Wole Soyinka. The most successful of these productions was *Oveye Na Matui Ahulili*, in which the passion of Christ was given a Maragoli setting. Three Third Formers, under the encouragement of Jill Claridge, the biology teacher, wrote the play in Luragoli, the tribal vernacular. With help from Miss Claridge and advice from David Cook of Makerere University College, the boys produced the play in the school hall with a simple set and elementary lighting, but with great enthusiasm. They then took it on tour to ten or more villages in the locations where it was an instant hit. The older people particularly were delighted to hear the more archaic version of their language and on occasion they were so caught up in the Easter theme, they spontaneously stood and took part in the action. The play then went on to Nairobi with a cast of twenty-four and technical assistance from John Inglis to sweep all three major prizes in the secondary section of the 1968 National Schools Drama Festival.

The play is an effective blending of the crucifixion theme and Maragoli custom. Muhonyi, a man of low birth, born in a local village, is beginning to upset the community with his teaching. Local elders become increasingly concerned over the challenge of this man to their authority, an authority they use, as do all men, to their own advantage. The local witch doctor is losing trade and is particularly incensed. The leaders plot the fall of Muhonyi, and the young man who betrays him is given an elder's beautiful daughter as his fourth wife. After his trial by a leading judge of the area, Muhonyi is condemned to be hacked to pieces and his body scattered to the hyenas. In the final scene he is dragged off to his execution, but soon returns in triumph. Although the adjudicators and the audience could not understand a word of Luragoli they recognized the play as authentic, indigenous drama that had been developed into a piece of moving theatre. It was also a sign that Chavakali boys have Maragoli roots which they want to keep watered. And the enthusiasm for the play in the villages revealed the lasting effects of the work of the Quaker missionaries. Christianity is now a part of Maragoli culture.

Although there is a modest religious emphasis in morning assembly and in a Sunday worship service, Chavakali is no longer a Friends' school. It was Quaker initiative, both local and American, which started the school, and as the first managers of Chavakali, the mission loaned the money to build staff houses, workshops, and laboratories in order to house the ICA staff and enable the new project to get started. But under education ordinances dating from 1952 and legislation culminating in the Education Act of 1968, all secondary schools were placed under the direction of boards of governors who in turn were responsible to the Minister of Education. No longer were the missions to serve as managers of secondary schools. The recruitment of staff at Chavakali is also no longer the responsibility of African or American Friends. If the Teachers Service Commission cannot fill a vacancy from local sources, the Ministry of Education, through its representatives in the United Kingdom, the United States, Canada, and elsewhere recruits expatriate teachers. Direct contact between a headmaster and organizations abroad is no longer permitted and he is obliged to accept teachers who are posted to him. Similarly, headmasters tend to be posted to boards of governors rather than selected by them. The two most recent headmasters of Chavakali were not Friends, and both were unfamiliar with the work of the East Africa Yearly Meeting.

The school-community relationship through agriculture is also more tenuous than in the school's early years. Now that almost all the boys are boarding, they no longer have demonstration plots on their home farms, and methods learned in agriculture courses do not seep into local practice as they once did. The school demonstration plots are of course available to the community, and on them local and hybrid maize are grown side by side under similar conditions. The present agriculture teacher, Fred Wawire, is able to produce nearly treble the yield from hybrid seed. The agriculture syllabus was revised in 1967 but the main topics of crop and animal husbandry, farm management, and farm mechanics still provide the structure of the four-year course. Wawire is an S1 teacher with a diploma from Egerton Agricultural College. In addition to teaching all the four years of agriculture, he supervises the school farm of 12 acres, advises the Young Farmers Club, and attempts to keep the tractor and other pieces of farm machinery in good repair. But he knows that the central purpose of his work is not to give Chavakali the flavor of a rural American high school or to demonstrate modern cultivation to Maragoli farmers, but to get Chavakali boys through their School Certificate.

## Chavakali's Dilemmas

IF an experimental school with a special function is to have any chance of success, it should have some continuity of leadership. Chavakali has had five headmasters in eight years. And if the school staff is to develop a feeling of unity and a sense of common purpose, there should be a limited turnover of teachers. In an average year staff turnover at Chavakali is 50 per cent. Thomas Howes, an able and dedicated headmaster who had formerly been a successful geography teacher in a London secondary school, came to Chavakali in 1968, totally unfamiliar with the basic notions that prompted the creation of the school. Even a year as a teacher in another secondary school in Kenya did not prepare him for the particular problems of Chavakali. And of the thirteen teachers on the staff (seven British, three Asian, two African, and one American) only one had been at the school during the period of the AID-Earlham contract. This was Philip Towle, a Quaker from New Hampshire, who has served the school wth a passionate commitment as building superintendent and physics teacher and has given a one-man continuity to the principles on which Chavakali was founded.

The total grant from the Kenya Government for operating the school in 1968 was £16,440, or about £60 per boy. The school charges fees for tuition and boarding of 620/ a year, and out of this revenue it must provide meals and hostel accommodation The diet is simple and, as in all African secondary schools, the boys are fed for less than 2/ per day. Boys who cannot pay fees are able to secure bursaries for which they work in the dining hall or in the school grounds for the equivalent of 7¢ (USA) an hour. The Government grant covers all staff salaries and the maintenance of school buildings and equipment. Equipment bought with the AID grant is now showing signs of deterioration and it is difficult to secure sufficient funds from Gill House to make replacements.

The influence of Chavakali on secondary education in Kenya will be deep and lasting because it revealed what local self-help could achieve and because it made a major breakthrough in curriculum reform. And yet, throughout its first decade, the school has lived from one crisis to another, and its achievements have not matched its potential. Its influence lies more in the Chavakali idea than in the Chavakali reality, and as an institutional model its troubled history is almost more useful in illustrating what to avoid than in demonstrating what to adopt. Yet it cannot be denied that it was at this school where the idea of teaching agriculture and industrial arts was successfully translated into a reality.

Here then is a school that as an institution has never really lived up to its promise. It could have been a new kind of rural high school emphasizing practical subjects for boys who would not go on to further education, and serving as a community demonstration centre for improving agriculture. To achieve these ends it needed sustained help from abroad, continuously strong leadership, and the adequate training and induction of African staff. Instead, the AID contract was awarded to a liberal arts college with no experience in providing technical assistance in agriculture and was concluded in less than four years before the experiment was given a fair trial. The school began under a colonial administration which accepted it reluctantly and then gave it minimum support. These attitudes towards the school persisted after Independence, when the Ministry continued to judge secondary schools by their Cambridge results. Although the latter were not good in the early years, they gradually improved, as did staff and student morale, under David Hunter, who was a deeply sensitive and creative headmaster from 1964 to 1966. In 1967, 84 per cent of the Fourth Form secured their School Certificates and Chavakali retained its "A" rating with the Cambridge Syndicate. For a school that selects its boys locally and does not have the advantage of national selection enjoyed by the secondary boarding schools, this is an impressive achievement. But to its American founders it means Chavakali is being measured with the wrong instrument.

On the other hand, the Earlham group was naïve to expect that the essential features of an American rural high school could be transplanted to the Maragoli locations. In the early '60's Kenya was not prepared to accept a high school savoring of the Midwest. It was, nevertheless, willing to admit agriculture and industrial arts into the secondary school curriculum, but at a price—they must become part of the School Certificate system. This in turn led to Chavakali's basic paradox. The Maragolis taxed themselves to start a school and, with considerable pride, have continued to think of it as their own. But to a Maragoli father the school has failed if his boy does not get his Certificate, which is his ticket-of-leave from the community. And in preparing for the examinations the boys and their teachers are so preoccupied they have little time or energy left to relate the school to Maragoli life. Chavakali, nevertheless, has made an impact. In 1964 the Kenya Government requested the expansion of agricultural teaching to other secondary schools. USAID responded to the request, and under a contract with the University of West Virginia, six American teachers were recruited and assigned to as many rural secondary schools with Robert Maxwell as chief of party. Each school was provided with a combination workshop-classroom, and equipment including a tractor at a cost of £7,575. The Government of Kenya agreed to pay recurrent costs, a part of which were to be used in developing school farms ranging in size from 5 to 15 acres. By 1966 nearly 1,000 students were enrolled in the agriculture course, and six Kenyans, who had completed the diploma course at Egerton Agricultural College, began counterpart training under the supervision of the USAID teachers. Kenya is now officially committed to teaching agriculture and it is expected that forty to fifty secondary schools will be participating by 1972. Expansion will be determined by the supply of teachers and the availability of funds. Egerton has added a teacher education option to its curriculum and forty-five students now enroll each year for the three-year course. But capital and recurrent costs are stickier problems. IDA loan funds will equip fourteen schools at probable capital expenditure of £5,000 per school, but foreign aid from other sources is unlikely to be sufficient to equip thirty more schools. And annual costs of close to £1,000 for a double-stream school will deter the expansion of the program. Nevertheless, now that agriculture is a recognized subject, it may be possible to devise ways of reducing equipment costs without sacrificing the essential features of the course. If, as has been predicted,[4] 5,000 Kenya young people are studying agriculture by 1972, the promise of Chavakali will be fulfilled.

[4] *Report of the Agricultural Education Commission* (Nairobi: Government Printer, 1967), p. 94.

[CHAPTER NINE]

# The Education of Secondary Teachers: Kenya Science Teachers College

## A Model of External Aid

POSSIBLY the most dramatic statistic ever produced by the Ministry of Education revealed that in 1966 the number of Kenyan graduates teaching secondary school science was three. Throughout the sixties the supply of qualified teachers (expatriate and local) did not keep pace with the booming enrollments of the secondary schools, but it was the proportion of Kenyans to expatriates that African leaders found most disturbing. Early in the decade, before Independence in fact, the Ministry of Education had realized that a source of secondary teacher supply, other than graduates, had to be found. The country could not wait five years (two in the sixth form and three in university) for what at best would be a thin trickle of graduate teachers. A new training scheme began in 1963 when some thirty-five students holding a School Certificate began a three-year course at the Central Teacher Training College in Nairobi. It was the beginning of nongraduate secondary teacher preparation. Five years later the enrollment had grown to 800 in two colleges whose chief function is to produce S1's, a new breed of teacher.

At Kenyatta College and the Kenya Science Teachers College, the S1 course is a blend of academic study and professional training. Over three years a student spends roughly two-thirds of his (or her) time in carrying two subjects to the equivalent of Higher School Certificate level, and the remainder in a combination of educational theory and teaching practice. With his S1 Certificate he is eligible to teach his main subject to Form IV level and, given the exigencies of secondary school staffing, another subject in Forms I and II. From the beginning it was assumed that S1's would be bonded to serve as secondary teachers for at least three years. Whether the program is a temporary measure until the supply of graduates is adequate, or a semipermanent scheme that will train teachers for the maintained and *harambee* schools for at least a generation, it is impossible to tell. Meanwhile the course has been somewhat ambiguously described as "the most realistic emergency solution in the long run."

Kenyatta College opened in 1965 in a garden suburb 10 miles from Nairobi, a gift from the British Government and formerly the Templar Barracks. The magnificent installation, the most extensive and best equipped of all British Army posts, was built in 1959 to accommodate and train a Mediterranean–Indian Ocean strategic reserve. It now has two divisions, a secondary school that will soon become a Sixth Form college, and a teacher training division concerned primarily with the training of S1's. By 1970 when it is expected that the administrative chaos of the early years will have cleared away and the two divisions will become an integrated unit, the college will have a total enrollment of some 1,200 students.

The other centre for S1 training is a gift from Sweden. It is in fact one of the most imaginative and carefully conceived gifts that Kenya has thus far received from a single donor, and certainly the most ambitious technical assistance project that Sweden has undertaken. A full year before Independence, a Swedish team had arrived in Kenya to discuss the implications of *Uhuru* for education. The result was a study entitled *Svensk hogskola i Afrika* (*A Swedish College in Africa*), completed in December, 1962, which in turn was followed in less than a year by an informal and exploratory request for assistance.[1]

---

[1] *Request for Swedish Assistance for a Science Institute in Nairobi*, October, 1963 (in the files of the Kenya Science Teachers College).

The request stressed the small number of science teachers of "local origin" and assumed that it would take ten years before any significant number of local graduate teachers of science could be produced. Meanwhile, what Kenya needed was a new institute to train science teachers on the S1 pattern already begun at Central Training College. After ten years, when a more adequate supply of graduates would be available, the institute should be converted into a junior college that would feed graduates into the science faculties of the University of East Africa. A close liaison with University College, Nairobi, should be established from the outset with reciprocity in research facilities and opportunity for the most able S1's to be admitted to UCN for a degree course. This request and its later modifications were largely the work of Dr. Ake Vinterback, who envisaged a project that would be built, staffed, equipped, and supported by Sweden for ten years. As Kenya gradually assumed responsibility both for staffing and maintenance, the college should become a part of the university system of East Africa. Its purpose would be primarily to train science teachers but it could also be expected to make an impact on science teaching throughout the secondary schools of Kenya. This could be done through staff participation in curriculum revision, the production of science apparatus, and refresher courses for teachers. It was a bold and imaginative proposal, and with only a few modifications, it gave shape and substance to the development of the Kenya Science Teachers College.

Why should Sweden offer to assist a developing country in an enterprise that by 1976 will probably have cost her $10 million? Clearly Sweden is not looking for allies in what used to be called the Cold War, and is not searching for projects that will open up trade outlets. Her aid is untied and there is no stipulation that Swedish products must be used in projects abroad. There may, of course, be a twinge of guilt in Sweden's desire to help the have-not nations, but a more probable explanation is the practical, no-nonsense concern of the Swedes to do something to reduce the widening gap between the rich and poor nations of the world. The social and economic policy that persuaded Sweden to develop a high level of social welfare at home has been transferred to the international scene, and a symbol of this may lie in the appointment in 1965 of Dr. Ernst Michanek, formerly Permanent Secretary in the Department of Social Sciences, to head the Swedish International Development Authority. In 1967-1968 SIDA had a modest budget of $50 million and was giving assistance in education, family planning, and food supply in six countries: Ethiopia, India, Kenya, Pakistan, Tanzania, and Tunisia. In addition, Sweden collaborates with international organizations in providing multilateral aid, and in proportion to population she has been one of the most generous contributors to the International Development Association of the World Bank.

If the criteria for aiding a new nation should include the meeting of a genuine need, the outright gift of buildings and equipment, the supply of high-level expertise, the gradual takeover of recurrent costs by the host country, and the planned phase out of the donor, then KSTC is a model of international cooperation. With characteristic thoroughness the Swedish Ambassador to Kenya negotiated an agreement with the Kenya Government in May, 1965, and thus far no changes have been necessary. On a site of 35 acres provided by the Kenya Government 4 miles from the centre of Nairobi, Sweden would supervise the building and pay 90 per cent of the cost of a residential college able to accommodate some 300 students, their teachers, and a maintenance staff. For the first five years Sweden would provide all teaching staff, and from 1971 to 1976 Kenyans would gradually replace Swedes. It was recognized that Kenyan counterparts would need to be educated and trained, either in Kenya or abroad, and Sweden agreed to award scholarships for the training. Sweden would pay the major share of recurrent costs in the early years of the agreement, and the Government of Kenya would increase its contribution to operating expenses according to this timetable:

| Year | Per Cent |
|------|----------|
| 1966–1970 | 30 |
| 1970–1972 | 50 |
| 1972–1973 | 60 |
| 1973–1974 | 70 |
| 1974–1975 | 80 |
| 1975–1976 | 90 |
| 1976 | 100 |

Instruction would be conducted in English, and the subjects to be offered were mathematics, physics, chemistry, biology, geography, English, and education. On the completion of their course, S1's would be expected to teach for at least three years. The Ambassador was careful to include a paragraph which kept the door of University College open to the cream of KSTC's output.

Even before the signing of the agreement SIDA had delegated most of the administration and staffing of the project to Uppsala University, and throughout 1965 various experts were at work developing syllabuses and drawing up lists of equipment. A staff of five was recruited by Uppsala, and in March, 1966, in temporary quarters in the former Central Training College, KSTC opened with an enrollment of forty-eight students. Two years later, and precisely on time, the new premises were ready. Designed by Graham McCullough, a Nairobi architect, and built under Swedish supervision, the concrete buildings lie rather heavily and without color in their not-too-spacious grounds. But everything else is done on a generous scale. Each student has his own study-bedroom and each member of staff his own house and office. There is an adequate library, a lecture theater seating 100, and an auditorium for 450. Classrooms and laboratories are well equipped, the workshop is fully stocked with hand and power tools, and the language laboratory has spaces for sixteen students. There are seventy-five housing units for all levels of staff, and beyond these stretch the playing fields and tennis courts. The landscape architect was H. P. Greensmith, who earned an international reputation as the designer of Nairobi's public gardens.

The visitor who attends classes in the new college is immediately struck by the competence of the staff and the quality of the facilities. A chemistry teacher enters the room and the class stands to exchange "good morning." It is a review lesson on the structure of the atom, and the text used is an American publication, *Chemistry, An Experimental Science*, prepared by the CHEM Study Project under a grant from the National Science Foundation. The teacher had become familiar with this new approach to chemistry during a year at Swarthmore College as a graduate student in 1964. Before coming to Kenya, he had taught in Sweden in a combined teachers college and secondary school. His English is excellent, he uses the blackboard skillfully, and teaches with warmth and confidence. Throughout the period the class of twenty-five (men and women, Asians and Africans) give him rapt attention and alternately take notes and raise questions. The tone and technique are closer to secondary school than a college, but the class atmosphere is dignified and mature. The classroom is tiered and can be darkened as needed; an overhead projector stands in one corner. Blackboards, cupboards, and a demonstration table are all of good size, and a periodic chart of the elements almost covers the back wall. In short, with its adjoining laboratory it appeared to be a thoroughly satisfactory setting in which to teach and learn chemistry.

### *Agents of Change*

IT is probably fair to say that the majority of KSTC students are themselves the products of schools in which teachers dictated notes and crammed their students for the Cambridge examinations. With its able staff and ample facilities the college intends to produce teachers who will break with traditional methods of teaching secondary school science. The educational philosophy of the college was revealed in this observation by one of the college's administrative officers:

> Science . . . began as natural philosophy and gradually settled down to become a course of scientific knowledge which was mainly factual and descriptive. The tradition of verbal learning and memorizing led to a formal and abstract approach, at the expense of practical work in laboratory and field and stimulating discoveries made by the students themselves. Knowing was thus often confused with remembering at the expense of understanding.[2]

One of the primary functions of KSTC is to prepare its students to teach the "new" science courses that have been developed in the last decade. For the staff this means putting emphasis on the academic rather than on the professional component of the S1 course on the assumption that the better an S1 knows his subject, the less authoritarian a teacher he will tend to be. But the college courses he takes must themselves not stress remembering at the expense of understanding. And the staff knows very well that their own example, their courses, and the way they teach them, will do more to persuade students towards a modern approach in teaching than any number of courses in educational theory. It is with this in mind that laboratory work, demonstrations, excursions, seminars, and independent study are given generous amounts of time. Lectures are rarely given, few notes are dictated, and classes are not rigidly structured. KSTC sums up its approach to teacher education in these terms:

> In many societies, traditions and customs have given the teacher an authority that sometimes has had an inhibiting effect on the interaction between teacher and student. No doubt the teacher should enjoy authority but it should come from the prestige that derives from social and intellectual leadership, rather than from autocratic traditions.
>
> KSTC seeks to realize these ideas in many ways, perhaps first of all through including in its teaching and extra-curricular ac-

---

[2] Olov Osterling, "The Educational Policy of KSTC," *Sunday Post* (Nairobi), May 26, 1968, p. 17.

tivities as many opportunities as possible for students to initiate action and to learn to become responsible by taking the lead. Realizing the fact that teachers tend to teach the way they themselves once were taught the College endeavours to give its own tuition the form of a cooperative effort in which the tutor is a work-leader, not a know-all, and the student a team-member, not a more or less inactive recipient of knowledge.[3]

In still another way the college attempts to modify African attitudes, particularly those relating to manual work. The young African grows up with few toys, usually none of a manipulative kind, and he associates tools with backbreaking work. An academic secondary education has done nothing to change his outlook, and he arrives at college with little skill and less enthusiasm for working with his hands. The college now faces the problem of changing his attitude and developing his dexterity so that he can manipulate laboratory equipment, demonstrate effectively, and use tools in the making of simple apparatus—all of which are necessary for the modern science teacher. Towards this end KSTC has built a workshop that extends along one full side of its classroom quadrangle. All students take a full-day workshop course for six weeks in their third year during which they work in wood and metal; learn techniques of welding, soldering, and glass blowing: and in the process make materials and equipment that are needed in science courses.

And finally, when the staff is asked to fill in the details of a portrait of the teacher as a young man—a picture of their product, they will mention such characteristics as endurance and commitment, the capacity to keep going under the difficult conditions of upcountry schools, together with a deep and abiding interest in their science subjects, and the determination to keep alive and growing in their field. They know, however, that their students will face opposition from teachers and pupils who place their trust in tested routines for passing Cam-

---

[3] *Ibid.*

bridge and are suspicious if not hostile towards the new science. KSTC students have already met such opposition in their teaching practice. One third-year physics major who had set up an experiment on color and was asking his class to make observations was interrupted by one of his students who said, "If you know what's going to happen, why waste our time? Tell us."

### Staff and Counterparts

IN recruiting staff Uppsala searches for the scholar who has a full command of his subject and an earned reputation as a teacher, who is fluent in English, flexible enough to thrive in a new college in a new country, and committed not only to his subject but to the job of training teachers. Thus far the search has been astonishingly successful. Dr. Olov Bergman, Principal from 1966 to 1968, is a nuclear physicist and former lecturer in physics at Uppsala who has done beta ray research for the American Aerospace Agency. His successor, Olov Osterling, is an educational psychologist who was formerly a department head in the Swedish National Board of Education. In 1968 fifteen of a staff of twenty-six had earned doctorates and a majority of the tutors were former secondary school teachers.

To obtain a high-quality staff Uppsala has mounted a national campaign and scheduled recruiting courses at which candidates are interviewed in depth and all aspects of the assignment are discussed. Those selected attend a month-long orientation course and are given intensive instruction in English and Swahili. The initial contract runs two years with an option to continue; of the first eleven staff appointments, seven asked to have their contracts renewed. Biology and geography tutors, who welcome experience in East Africa because it broadens their professional horizons and offers opportunity for research, are easier to recruit than chemists and physicists, who fear they may lose touch with their field.

The staff probably works harder at KSTC than they do at home. In addition to teaching, they supervise teaching practice, tutor students in their independent study projects, and occasionally lead excursions. All of this mounts up to a teaching load of twenty periods a week. They have developed their own syllabuses which have been approved by the senate of the university, and the way is finally clear for the more able S1's to secure admission to University College. Whenever possible, and this is particularly true in biology and geography, the courses are related to East Africa. The biology tutors for example, have developed a set of materials on "The Ecology and Ecosystems of Kenya," and the course in physical geography stresses concepts which are related to economic development in Africa, particularly in agriculture.

According to the agreement, the college will have a full Swedish staff until 1970. Four Kenyans will be appointed for the opening of the college year in March, 1971, and four more will be appointed each year thereafter until the staff is entirely Kenyan in 1976. This pace of Kenyanization can, however, be increased—if fully qualified tutors become available. This is highly unlikely if left to chance, and with characteristic efficiency and careful planning, the present college staff has launched a training scheme. A group of experienced P1 and S1 teachers were invited to the college for one week late in 1967 and given a battery of tests. Thirty survived the screening, and in January enrolled at KSTC for an intensive, full-time university preparatory course that will last for eighteen months. It is expected that perhaps fifteen to twenty will gain university entrance, and on completion of both the bachelor's and master's degree in science, they will return to the college as tutors. It is, in effect, a six-year training scheme that may possibly produce ten Kenya tutors by 1974.

Another source of supply will be that small but growing pool of science graduates of either the University of East Africa or universities abroad who have taught for several years in secondary schools. The KSTC staff is now searching for these graduate teachers and is prepared to give them assistance to pursue postgraduate study to the master's level either in East Africa, or, possibly, at Uppsala. The staff will also be watching the progress of the more promising of their own S1's. Those who reveal both high quality as teachers and academic potential will be assisted towards a degree and encouraged to become teacher trainers. The KSTC staff are, in short, identifying and nurturing those who will succeed them. There is, however, one snag that may frustrate all plans for the recruitment and training of counterparts: graduate tutors are now on the same salary scale as trained graduate teachers of secondary schools, and the range is from £810 to £1,710 per year. Furthermore, teaching experience is the sole factor in determining salary, and a tutor with a master's degree or a doctorate is paid no more than a B.A. Until tutor salaries are improved, there is little likelihood of recruiting Kenyans with training and ability comparable to the Swedes.

## The Three-Year Course

BECAUSE there are few precedents or guidelines in Africa for the education of nongraduate secondary teachers, KSTC has devised its own pattern of courses that will prepare an S1 to teach two subjects effectively to Form IV and, if need be, other science subjects in Forms I and II. A student plunges into fourteen-week introductory courses in all five sciences (mathematics, physics, chemistry, biology, and geography), which are designed to expand his general education in science and to help him decide the subjects in which he wants to concentrate. Throughout this period the emphasis is on instruction and he spends forty periods a week in classroom and laboratory. Then follow basic courses in three of the sciences for thirty-five weeks and, finally, higher courses in two subjects for forty-two weeks to complete the three-year program. With each section the amount of classroom and laboratory instruction decreases until it reaches fifteen hours a week at the beginning of the third year. Finally, a student embarks on a period of independent study. Supplementing the work in science are courses in English (with stress on oral and written usage), drawing, laboratory techniques, and the workshop courses. As a complement to what the Principal feels is a "heavily science-minded curriculum," there is time set aside for "general arts"—speakers and discussion on African literature, history, and current affairs. The intent, clearly, is to give a student both breadth and depth in the sciences, and at least a brush with the humanities.

The education courses fall mainly into the third year. The instructor in principles and practices of education, which is primarily a course in educational psychology, faces the problem of a very limited bibliography on the growth and development of African adolescents. In fact, research studies are only now beginning; in the meantime he is obliged to use American and British references. Instruction in teaching methods is the responsibility of each academic department. During both the second and third years, time is set aside for students to teach practice lessons to their peers in regular KSTC classes. These are discussed and criticized by the tutor and class and tape recorded for still further analysis. It is during this subject method course that students are introduced to the aims and techniques of teaching the new science curriculum, and *Teachers Guides* to the Nuffield courses are required reading. The willingness of the science departments to teach both content and method is one of KSTC's great strengths.

Teaching practice at KSTC is scheduled only in the third year but is regarded as a crucially important phase of the program. Before going out to their schools, students are coached carefully on the need for detailed planning and the importance of establishing good rapport both with pupils and supervising teachers. A thirty-seven–page manual *Guidelines and Suggestions for Teaching Practice* leaves nothing to chance. A student usually teaches two classes each day over two six-week sessions during which he has no classes at the college. Thus he can be at his school throughout the day and has time to observe other teachers. KSTC staff travel to the schools and observe their students once a week in each of their two teaching subjects. The college is attempting a variety of means to create a partnership with its cooperating schools. The most able and imaginative teachers are sought as supervisors, invited to the college for consultation, and regarded as colleagues in the training process. Some of these supervisors will no doubt find their way into upgrading courses that the college will offer to in-service teachers during vacation periods, and a few, particularly if they are African, may be chosen for further study and marked for posts as tutors on the KSTC staff.

## The Students

ADMISSION to KSTC is not a private affair between the college and an applicant. Halfway through the school year all Fourth Formers in Kenya schools are required to fill out a detailed document on which they list their preferences for the next year, and their headmasters provide a judgment of their ability and character. When School Certificate results are available, the National Directorate of Personnel uses these forms and attempts to match student preferences, Cambridge results, and manpower needs. This means that Form V places are filled first by students who showed a preference for Form V and secured a Division I school certificate. (Students may, of course, refuse a Form V place, but few do, as this is the pathway to the university.) Teacher training places are offered next, followed by positions in Government departments, and jobs in private business and industry. KSTC is obliged to operate within the framework of this system of selection, but it nevertheless recruits vigorously, sending its staff and brochures to secondary schools, and losing no opportunity to be mentioned in press and radio. It encourages students to come for an interview and to make preliminary application directly to the college. In these ways it has managed to increase the number who apply for a place at the college, and, in turn, it has probably improved the quality of its selection. About 20 per cent of students entering in 1968 had Division I School Certificates, and all others had Division II. The college is also experimenting with a battery of tests (abstract and verbal reasoning, and mathematics) and over a period of time will correlate the results with performance in college courses. Such tests may possibly prove to be better instruments of selection than School Certificate grades.

When the new buildings opened in March, 1968, the planned annual entry of 100 was admitted. The enrollment then was as follows:

|  | Men | Women | Total |
|---|---|---|---|
| First year | 83 | 16 | 99 |
| Second year | 34 | 12 | 46 |
| Third year | 37 | 3 | 40 |
| P1-S1 counterpart course | 27 | — | 27 |
| Enrolled at Uppsala | 2 | — | 2 |
| Total | 183 | 31 | 214 |

Since 1967 all entering students have been Kenya citizens, and, of course, Africans outnumber Asians. Students themselves testify that genuine integration exists at KSTC and that brown and black students mingle freely and comfortably not only in classes but in the common room and on the playing fields. Since the college opened its doors there have been no racial incidents.

By training college standards, particularly those of primary training colleges, the students of KSTC are not shackled by regulations. They may leave the campus during week ends simply by signing out with the duty master, and on weekdays they come and go pretty well as they please. The only major restriction is a blanket out-of-bounds rule forbidding men and women to visit each other's residences. Otherwise, students are treated as mature adults. Student life tends to be simple and Spartan. The food budget, a part of Kenya's contribution to operating expenses, is limited to an allowance of 2/50 per student per day. This means that in the midst of lush surroundings, the diet tends to be uninspired.

There are no tuition fees and no charges for board, room, or books. Every student receives a cash allowance of 120/ at the beginning of the college year and 15/ per month thereafter. Frequently, this allowance is all the spending money a student will have. The morale of students appears to be high. They are deeply grateful to Sweden not only for the equipment and amenities of KSTC but probably even more for dedicated and effective teaching. Third-year students have begun to organize an Old Boys Association. Although a good proportion of students may have accepted a training-college place as a consolation prize when they realized Form V entry was out of their reach, they now appear to be reconciled to, and even enthusiastic about, teaching. And they have a Cause, the building of a new nation, and, unlike students in more developed societies, they are not suffering from alienation and disaffection. Here is the Student Council president summing up his faith:

> We are going out into a tough and stormy world, but with the hope that victory can be won over evil forces that threaten us. Easy-going pessimism is fatal. What we need is intelligence, faith, goodwill and courage. We must not believe that this universe is as one materialist put it "all an affair of chance; the froth and fume of waves on an ocean of sterile matter." There is mind behind our life here, meaning and purpose running through it, and destiny ahead of it.[4]

## Impact

OVER the decade 1970–1980 KSTC will produce some 1,000 science teachers. Assuming a wastage or dropout from teaching

---

[4] *Kenya Science Teachers College Magazine* (Nairobi: 1967), p. 65.

of 5 per cent a year the number of KSTC S1's still teaching in 1980 should stand at about 800, or enough to staff the science courses in 300 secondary school streams.[5] In addition, the college will probably have branched out into the preparation of industrial arts teachers, and will have given an unpredictable number of vacation courses for in-service teachers. On the other hand, it may have changed its complexion and become one of the constituent colleges of the University of Kenya. But whatever its future it has already had an impact and influence on teacher education and secondary school science teaching in Kenya. Its S1 syllabuses for physics, chemistry, and biology have been adopted by the Teacher Training Division of Kenyatta College, and its staff have participated in several phases of the work of the Kenya Institute of Education, particularly those related to training-college curriculums and the science syllabuses for secondary schools.

The driving force in these early years has been Olov Bergman. It was his energy, thoroughness, practicality, and high intelligence that gave the college its tone of efficiency and brought its staff and students together with a sense of purpose. Bergman and his highly effective deputy, Lars Bjorkman, and their staff could have created a little Sweden with an annual output of teachers and few connections beyond the campus. Instead, they have managed, with both Swedish charm and intensity, to identify their project with Kenya and to integrate it fully into Kenya's educational system. KSTC is now a part of the teacher training complex, its staff and facilities are inspected, and its students' teaching practice assessed by the inspectorate and the KIE. But it is also a model, and with its new building, energetic administration, and competent staff, it has given an *élan* to teacher education, and certainly a respectability and good name to the training of nongraduate secondary teachers.

---

[5] Here the term "stream" refers to four classes—Form I to Form IV. Each stream requires the equivalent of two and two-thirds science (mathematics, physics, chemistry, biology, and geography) teachers.

But hard times lie ahead. Below the surface of Sweden's generosity lies a basic belief in Kenya's capacity not simply to take over the college but to maintain its present high standards of staff and equipment. This will mean an intensification of counterpart training and a recognition that both academic qualifications and salaries for African tutors will have to be moved well beyond present levels. Otherwise, KSTC will fall into the mediocrity that has marked so much of teacher training in East Africa. The recurrent cost of educating a student at KSTC will be much nearer that of University College than a training college—if tutors' salaries are raised and if buildings and equipment are maintained at present standards. In 1966 the annual costs of maintaining a student in a primary training college and at the university were, respectively, £140 and £1,130.[6] Because of the present complexity of KSTC's financing, it is difficult to estimate accurately the recurrent cost per student. Nevertheless, a rough estimate by the Principal gives a figure of £750. With an enrollment of 300 students the college is, clearly, going to be expensive for Kenya to maintain. A possible relief from this burden could take the form of student loans. As high- and middle-level manpower quotas are filled and teaching becomes a more attractive profession—simply because there are fewer other career opportunities—it should be possible to charge fees and offer loans rather than give students full tuition and maintenance.

A further problem relates to teaching practice. In its early years the college sent its students to five cooperating schools all of which are in Nairobi and environs. With the increasing number of students in training at Kenyatta College, University College, and KSTC, the schools of Nairobi will find that they cannot accept all the demands made on them for teaching practice. Up- and down-country schools will have to be used and KSTC staff will be hard put to maintain their supervision schedule of observing each student once a week in each of his

---

[6] James R. Sheffield (ed.), *Education, Employment and Rural Development* (Nairobi: East African Publishing House, 1967), p. 275.

subjects. The college has foreseen this dilemma and is considering an internship plan under which students will live at school and teach on salary for a term, perhaps longer, in their third year. The major responsibility for supervision would be with the headmaster and his staff, with college tutors making only occasional visits.

The present S1 course may be a temporary stopgap, or "the most realistic emergency solution in the long run," or a permanent feature of teacher training in Kenya. Much will depend on Kenya's plan of educational development and whether or not she continues to place high priority on the expansion of secondary schools. It is, however, doubtful if the hunger of Kenya parents for a secondary education for their children will abate, and even more doubtful that the supply of graduate science teachers will be sufficient to replace S1's. Under these predictions KSTC will not become a college in the university system as now constituted, and its role will continue to lie in producing a good brand of S1's.

Its influence will lie at a deeper level than staffing science classrooms. The college is a new kind of missionary enterprise and the good word it brings is about science. Not, however, a science that is a series of abstractions to be verbalized and facts to be remembered, but a science that is based on inquiry and experiment, observation and discovery. This implies an approach to teaching that is analytical rather than descriptive, and a course content that in biology, for example, conveys some of the basic principles underlying living phenomena. And courses in physics in which students learn how to *do* physics, and to solve problems by recognizing the concepts that underlie each problem. For the majority of African children thinking like a scientist is a new way of life, and a way that is encouraged by Kenya's leaders, particularly her Chief Education Officer:

> The economic and social development of Kenya depends on our producing in the educational system men and women equipped with a basic understanding of scientific principles.

... Science teaching in schools involves far more than teaching useful scientific facts and knowledge of natural phenomena. Quite as important a task is to liberate the minds of the young from irrational beliefs, to encourage them to inquire about the nature of things and give positive attitudes concerning the ability of men and women to shape and control their environment to meet their needs. Science represents more than a corpus of knowledge that a few of our students need: it involves a whole approach to life which all our young people should be encouraged to share.[7]

KSTC and its staff are missionaries of this approach to life and in the years since Independence, Kenya has been open to their message.

[7] Kyale Mwendwa, *Kenya Science Teachers College Magazine*, I, 1967, p. 9.

## PART FOUR. THE WAY AHEAD

[CHAPTER TEN]

*Pressures, Constraints, and
New Directions*

KENYA's accomplishments in education have been remarkable. In the first five years of independence the guard changed almost completely within the Ministry of Education as an African administration took over, the number of primary school leavers doubled, secondary school enrollment trebled, and a new spirit began to permeate school and training college classrooms. But the purpose of this chapter is not to extol Kenya's educational accomplishments. It is, rather, to scout the road ahead, examine some of the major obstacles, and raise the question of whether a change in direction is needed.

*The Population Problem*

BEHIND all the advance that Kenya has achieved in education and social welfare, there lies the spectre of unplanned population growth. The facts can be swiftly told in these statistics.

>Present life expectancy is forty-five years and rising.
>The average Kenya woman has seven children.
>The rate of population increase is close to 3 per cent
>    per year—a rate among the highest in the world.
>Nearly half the population is less than fifteen years
>    of age.

At the request of the Government of Kenya an advisory mission of the Population Council of the United States visited

Kenya in 1965 to study the population problem. After visiting many parts of the country and considering all aspects of the problem, the mission recommended a national family planning program that would attempt to reduce fertility by as much as 50 per cent in ten to fifteen years. In its report the team revealed only too vividly the implications of population growth for education.

TABLE I *

*Projected Primary School Age Population of Kenya 1965–1990 Compared to Enrollment under Two Assumptions Regarding Fertility*

|  | Population Age 6–12 (Thousands) | | School Enrollment (Thousands) Assumed 4 Per Cent Annual Rate of Increase | Population Age 6–12 Not Enrolled (Thousands) | |
|---|---|---|---|---|---|
|  | Fertility Unchanged | Fertility Reduced by 50 Per Cent in Fifteen Years |  | Fertility Unchanged | Fertility Reduced by 50 Per Cent in Fifteen Years |
| 1965 | 1,760 | 1,760 | 970 | 790 | 790 |
| 1970 | 2,060 | 2,060 | 1,180 | 880 | 880 |
| 1975 | 2,430 | 2,250 | 1,430 | 1,000 | 820 |
| 1980 | 2,910 | 2,380 | 1,740 | 1,170 | 640 |
| 1985 | 3,480 | 2,270 | 2,120 | 1,360 | 150 |
| 1990 | 4,170 | 2,220 | 2,580 | 1,590 | 0 |

* *Family Planning in Kenya* (Nairobi: Government Printer, 1967), p. 5.

The implications to be found in Table I are striking. In 1965 some 55 per cent of primary age children were in school; in 1990 only 62 per cent would be in school—if fertility remains unchanged. On the other hand, *if fertility were to be reduced by 50 per cent in fifteen years, all children would be in school shortly after 1985.* Perhaps even more striking is the fact that with maintained high fertility the number of *illiterate, that is, unschooled children would double in the next twenty-five years.*

Any hope of achieving universal primary education without reducing the rate of population growth is remote. With fertility unchanged and at a current capital cost of £20 per primary school place, it would cost £100 million to build the additional schools needed to educate all primary age children at the end of the century. In an analysis of the educational and social implications of the population problem the *Development Plan* somberly concludes, "If the objective of universal primary education is to be realized in a reasonable period without seriously jeopardizing economic growth, the rapid rate of population growth must be checked. Similar considerations apply to the attainment of universal medical care and other social objectives." [1] The Government of Kenya has taken a positive stand on population control and has mounted a program of family planning with its own resources (some £20,000 a year) and larger contributions from foreign donors. New clinics have been opened and by mid-1968 these had a clientele of some 1,000 women per month. It has been estimated that a program designed to reduce the birth rate by 40 per cent in ten years would cost £160,000 a year and would involve a network of clinics serving 150,000 new users of contraceptives each year.

## Political and Social Pressures

THE people of Kenya and their representatives in the National Assembly have not forgotten Kenya African National Union's promise of free universal primary education. This question and the matter of secondary school places are probably the most frequently discussed issues in domestic politics. But in spite of

---

[1] *Kenya Development Plan 1965–66 to 1969–70* (Nairobi: Government Printer, 1966), p. 52.

the pressures, the Government has been very cautious. It realizes that there is no such thing as "free" education, and if a million more children were put to school and if the £3 million now collected from parents in school fees were shifted to local taxation, the result would be a heavier financial burden than the local authorities could stand. Furthermore, any rapid increase in enrollment would almost certainly bring a deterioration in the quality of primary education. It has proved difficult to maintain staffing standards even under the modest enrollment increases of recent years, and, in spite of attempts at upgrading, 30 per cent of all primary teachers were still untrained in 1967. The Kenya Government has accepted the Ominde Commission's view that educational standards must not give way "before the irresistible force of numbers" and has placed high priority on teacher training and the in-service education of primary teachers.

But political and social pressures will continue for both more primary and secondary schooling. The unaided secondary schools constitute a national problem of major proportions. In 1967 comparative figures were these:

| Aided Schools | | Unaided Schools | |
| --- | --- | --- | --- |
| Schools | Pupils | Schools | Pupils |
| 206 | 49,488 | 336 | 39,291 |

The *harambee* schools represent a long and strong tradition of self-help and symbolize the faith of African families in the investment value of education. But these families expect that the education offered will be of a kind that they can understand, and thus the schools have adopted the academic and literary traditions of the aided schools and give even greater emphasis to examinations and certificates. For the majority of the schools that will not be brought into the aided system the future looks bleak. Their school committees and boards of governors will favour little deviation from the academic curriculum, and attempts to relate the schools to rural reconstruction will probably be resisted. Furthermore, the financial stringencies facing the schools allow for only minimum facilities. At a conference sponsored in August, 1966, by the Education Department of University College, Nairobi, and attended by some fifty *harambee* school headmasters it was found that only eight of their schools had laboratories, ten had libraries, and essential texts were available for only half of their students.[2]

It can be argued that the need for fees is itself a stimulus to effort that benefits the economy, and keeping children in *harambee* schools is at least a partial solution of the primary school leaver problem. But these schools are attracting the better qualified teachers away from primary schools and not infrequently moving into primary school buildings. They have neither the equipment nor the staff to offer agriculture, industrial arts, or commercial subjects and hence concentrate on preparing their students for the academic options of the Kenya Junior School Certificate examination which is taken at the end of Form II. Many of the evils of the School Certificate system are now appearing at a lower level as students try to cram their way through the KJSC examinations.

If the results of these examinations are any test of the quality of the *harambee* schools, the misgivings of the Ominde Commission were justified: in 1967 only 35 per cent of their candidates secured passes in five subjects. Parents who have sacrificed so much to send their children to these schools can only be disappointed with the results, and if, as is likely, School Certificate results are no better, political repercussions will probably be serious.

The Ministry of Education is, however, ready to rescue at least a proportion of the *harambee* schools by bringing them into the maintained system. In a major change of policy the Ministry decided in 1967 to concentrate in the period 1968–1970, the second phase of the development program, on aiding one-stream rural secondary schools, eighty of which would be

---

[2] John E. Anderson, *Report on the Conference of Harambee School Headmasters* (Nairobi: 1966), mimeographed.

*harambee*. This decision will soften political pressures by providing a wider geographical distribution of secondary schools, and by taking the first step towards unifying the unaided and aided systems. But on educational grounds it is questionable. A one-stream school cannot offer a wide range of subjects because of staff limitations, and cannot justify the expense of workshops and equipment for teaching practical subjects. Nor does it normally attract specialist teachers. In the light of a good deal of testimony, the Ominde Commission urged that all investment capital for secondary education be concentrated on building up existing day schools to three streams and boarding schools to four streams. On the other hand, the one-stream day school is the least expensive to operate, and a good deal of capital expenditure will be saved by taking over buildings that were constructed under the impetus of self-help.

There may be other options for incorporating at least some of the more flexible *harambee* schools into the educational system. If they were to concentrate on Forms I and II only and prepare their students for KJSC rather than the School Certificate, they would be aiming at a more realistic goal. Following Form II, the most able students would be admitted to Form III places in the maintained schools or in a centrally located *harambee* school which was adequately equipped to offer Forms III and IV. If both the public and private sector can be persuaded to recognize the KJSC as a qualification for employment or a means of entry to vocational and technical training, the average *harambee* school leaver would then be able to find his way into business and industry. Or better still, if the range of subjects could be broadened and a new emphasis given to the teaching of present subjects the schools would speak more directly to the needs of rural youth:

> Basic subjects such as English and Mathematics need to be taught so that they can be used . . . in such tasks as the keeping of accounts of a farm, writing up a proposal for a loan, reading a simple manual on motor car manufacture or fertilizers, selecting paperback books for further education, and being

able to act as a secretary or treasurer to a local development committee. Subjects such as history and geography need to be slanted much more towards social and economic conditions prevailing in the society the students are living in and to the requirements of citizenship. . . . Secondary school science should provide students with basic knowledge that will enable them to take an interest in farming, the processing of farm products . . . and the application of modern techniques.[3]

A third political problem has to do with the very unequal distribution of school places in various parts of the country. In 1965 some 90 per cent of the children in Central Province were enrolled in primary school, but only 45 per cent in Rift Valley and Coast Provinces, and 1 per cent in the North Eastern Province. Part of the reason for this inequality of opportunity is the sparse and nomadic population in some areas, but it is also due to the inability of local authorities to collect sufficient taxes to finance schools and other social services. In 1965 six county councils found it necessary to dismiss 3,000 teachers and close their schools. A system of central government grants to local authorities designed to equalize educational opportunity has been slow in emerging. Meanwhile, the more prosperous districts have had the most schools, and legislative and administrative procedures have perpetuated a familiar principle in education: "Unto him that hath shall be given."

## Economic Restraints

How much can Kenya afford to spend on education? In the two years 1965–1966 to 1967–1968 Ministry of Education expenditure increased by 40 per cent to a total of £6.8 million, and Kenya is now among the top spending nations in the world when education costs are calculated as a proportion of the gross domestic product. It is doubtful if that proportion can go higher (it is now about 7 per cent), and there are several fac-

---

[3] *Ibid.*, p. 12.

tors that will tend to restrain any marked increase in the education budget.

Kenya's economic growth is closely related to income from agriculture, and thus both adverse weather and a drop in the price level of primary products in world markets can have a considerable effect on Kenya's economy. A prolonged drought in 1965 and a drop in export prices for her chief products in 1967 have put a brake on economic growth. The economy had, in fact, by 1967 lagged behind the rate of growth projected by the Development Plan. In the five years following Independence Kenya received from abroad gifts, loans, and technical assistance almost sufficient to match the expectations of the Development Plan, but the present mood of the American Congress and the economic stringencies facing Britain are not encouraging signs from the two major donors. Furthermore, there has been an over-all shrinkage of assistance to developing countries in what was hopefully to be the Development Decade. In a trenchant address to the Economic Commission of Africa at Lagos in February, 1967, Tom Mboya, Minister of Economic Planning and Development, spoke of the decline in the flow of capital to the developing world and the growing gap between the rich nations and the poor:

> The first six years of the Development Decade have passed. It has been a period of disappointment bordering on failure, whether measured in terms of UN targets, expectations in developing countries, or possibilities as indicated by the wealth of the advanced countries. Over that period the average person in the wealthy countries improved his income by approximately $220 to $1,800 per annum while *per capita* income in the very poor nations advanced by perhaps $7 to $90 per annum. Admittedly the $7 could have been less, and it is therefore a measure of both slight accomplishment and major defeat. If progress continues at this rate we will be able in retrospect to rename the Development Decade the Dollar-A-Year Decade. That to me is an apt description of utter failure.[4]

---
[4] Tom Mboya, *A Development Strategy for Africa* (Nairobi: Government Printer, 1967), p. 2.

Kenya has committed herself to a very high level of recurrent expenditure for education, which at the present rate of economic growth she is going to find difficult to maintain. The largest item, of course, is teachers' salaries, and the figures climb inexorably upward each year as more teachers are employed, as qualifications improve, and as teachers, most of whom are comparatively young, move up the salary scale. The problem of meeting recurrent costs deepened when the Government recently announced a new schedule of teachers' salaries which provided increases in all categories. In 1966, education accounted for 20 per cent of the total expenditure of central and local government, and education costs have since risen proportionately faster than expenditure for other government services. Within the education budget the most difficult problem will be to maintain an adequate level of aid to the secondary schools. This now accounts for half of all Ministry of Education expenditure and is rising relentlessly because of Development Plan commitments.

Still another dilemma that continues to vex Kenya is the growing rate of unemployment, particularly among primary and secondary school leavers. Figures on unemployment are by no means accurate but the number of "hard core" unemployed—those who are landless and jobless—may exceed 20,000, and those "underemployed" in seasonal or casual jobs number many more, perhaps over a million. As wages have gone up more young people are attracted to the towns, particularly those whose aspirations have risen through the completion of a primary school education. Since 1965 some 150,000 boys and girls have poured out of Standard VII of the primary schools each year, and fewer than 25 per cent have found a job or a place in secondary schools of all types. Many jobs that were once open to primary leavers now require Form II or Form IV qualifications. Thus tens of thousands of youngsters eager to "take off" from the traditional to the modern sector have met frustration and disappointment. The school leaver problem is deepening into a crisis as not only the primary but secondary school leavers are unable to find work. In July, 1968, over 1,000 School Certificate holders were registered as without jobs by the Ministry of Labour. This situation developed as the localization of the Civil Service was achieved, and the output of the secondary schools outpaced the growth of wage employment in the private sector.

## Adaptation, African Style

THOMAS HARDY once remarked, "If a way to the better there be, it exacts a full look at the worst," and that is what we have done in examining, if only briefly, the constraints and pressures that are facing Kenya in her first decade of independence. And these must be reckoned with in building a strategy for educational development.

Kenya is an agricultural nation and the majority of her people can expect to continue to live and work on the land. Economic development depends on bringing an increasing number of small farmers into a modern and productive economy through a program of land redistribution and settlement, improvement of access roads, the encouragement of local processing industries, and an increase in the quantity and quality of cash crops. In short, what Kenya needs is an agrarian revolution because it is essentially in the agricultural sectors of the economy that income and employment can be created. (A shrewd economist has predicted that only one-fifth of Kenya's labor force will find jobs in urban areas in 1985, and less than 30 per cent by the turn of the century.) [5] The most effective way to persuade the school leaver to become a farmer is to show him that he can make money and enjoy a reasonable standard of living by farming. This evidence will be infinitely more persuasive than any attempts to develop a love of the

---

[5] O. D. K. Norbye, "Long Term Employment Prospects and the Need for Large-scale Rural Works Programmes," *Education, Employment and Rural Development*, ed. James R. Sheffield, *op. cit.*, p. 265.

land by making alterations in the primary school curriculum. The Uganda Education Commission expressed this view in paragraphs 106 and 107 of its report of 1963:

> Our first observation, then, is this; until there has been a substantial breakthrough from relatively unproductive subsistence land use to much more intensive and profitable forms of farming in which young people can see a return for their efforts, school leavers will continue to seek other means of employment. Hence, paradoxically, *the problems of agricultural education are not primarily educational;* they are intimately bound up with the solution of economic, technical, and social problems over which the Ministry of Education has no control —systems of land tenure, improved land use, finance and marketing, research and development, traditions and tribal customs being among them.

There is, however, here a dangerous assumption that education has no role to play in effecting a rural transformation. And this brings us to the heart of the problem because what is needed is a kind of education that will transmit the information, create the attitudes, and develop the skills from which the agricultural revolution will grow. It will include not only the more formal education of primary and secondary schools but adult literacy programs, agricultural extension, community development, youth programs, and on-the-job training—what Guy Hunter has called "educative services"—in the belief that it is mainly through the adult farmer that innovation will come and, through him, more opportunity for the young. Education can then be one of the chief tools in achieving a rural transformation if it assists the adult farmer to become more productive.

This will, however, mean a reappraisal of priorities in educational planning and, possibly, a reshaping of the educational system. As we have seen, the Development Plan for 1965–1970 stressed the need for high-level manpower and placed heavy emphasis on secondary, technical, and university education. The phenomenal increase in secondary school enrollment, partly by design, and partly under social and political pressures, has now created the reservoir from which middle- and high-level manpower can be selected and trained. That reservoir now appears to be full enough and it should be possible to divert funds towards a network of educative services in rural areas. Whether such a change would be politically feasible is another question which will be considered in a moment.

For the great majority of young people, education and training are needed between the leaving of primary school and the beginning of productive life as adults. Primary school leavers are increasingly going to be thirteen or fourteen years of age if the present age of entry to Standard I remains at six or seven. And they have no marketable skills. There are, therefore, two gaps—a gap of years and a gap of skills—that must be crossed if a primary school leaver is going to find employment or become self-employed as a modern farmer. To fill these gaps productively for those who are between the ages of fourteen and seventeen and not enrolled in a secondary school is one of Kenya's most urgent, if not explosive, problems. At present there are some informal channels of education and training—the 4K (rural youth) Clubs, Young Farmers Clubs, and youth centres—but more opportunities are needed. Here indeed is a new educational frontier, and priority formerly placed on secondary education might well be transferred to programs for rural youth.

One of the most imaginative proposals in this direction made by a joint working party of the Christian Council of Kenya and the Christian Churches Educational Association is the "Village Polytechnic." Using the premises of the youth centres and employing a staff of six, each Village Polytechnic would enroll one hundred young men and women each year for a two-year course. The emphasis would lie in teaching skills and practical techniques connected with making money. Artisan training in wood and metal would develop manual skills needed by the farmer, and students would learn farm techniques, and find how money can be made by following sound advice on both the Village Polytechnic plot and their own *shambas.* In addition they would learn down-to-earth, practical techniques of letter writing, bookkeeping, banking, and organizing village societies.

But practical training alone is not sufficient. A Kenya farmer lives by his wits as well as his hands, as he chooses which mixture of crops to plant, where each crop ought to be planted, and copes with price fluctuations, school fees, loan payments, and pregnant wives. He may have to make decisions and adjustments with respect to three food crops, two or more kinds of livestock, and three or more cash crops. As Jon Moris has demonstrated, the component of manual skill is less important than the farmer's technical knowledge.[6]

With a combination of practical training and technical instruction the Village Polytechnic has great promise, and at very modest cost. Each Village Polytechnic could be financed for as little as £1,500 a year with support coming from central and local government grants and student fees. Supplementary income might come from the sale of farm produce and community project work undertaken by students.

In any case, recurrent costs would be more similar to those of the primary rather than to the day secondary school which in 1966 were, respectively, £8 and £65 per student. The success of the scheme would depend largely on the quality of local leadership and the skill and dedication of the staff. For 125 Village Polytechnics with an enrollment of 25,000 students, 250 teachers and a similar number of agricultural and artisan instructors would need to be recruited and given a special course of training. Some staff would come from the present youth centres, but the majority would have to be recruited from other sources. It would not be impossible to secure external aid funds to train these instructors:

> Such a scheme would bring considerable benefits to the nation. The energies of about half each annual group of unemployed rural primary school leavers would be mobilized for two years

---

[6] Jon Moris, "Farmer Training as a Strategy for Rural Development," *op. cit.*, pp. 325–326.

and oriented towards profitable activity in their own localities. The agricultural revolution would be accelerated. Large numbers of young people would have had the aims and methods of the Development Plan—down to locational level—explained to them and they would be participating in its fulfillment. Some potential misfits and criminals would have been brought into the mainstream of the life of the community. The energies of teenage frustration would be diverted to social goals. The premises of the "Village Polytechnics" would be used for classes for the "unschooled", for adult literacy and education of all sorts, under various Community Development programs, and with voluntary leaders, recreational clubs might well flourish under various auspices. The processes of economic development and nation building would be speeded up, and the tide of the rural exodus would be significantly reduced. Thousands of individuals would find new opportunities for personal fulfillment. Tens of thousands of potential political malcontents would find new avenues for constructive work.[7]

When education is adapted, African style, to rural development (initially in a number of strategically placed pilot projects financed with foreign aid), and when evidence mounts that it is possible to make a decent living on the land, and when young people withdraw from the gamble of finding a job in town as they see there are prizes to be won at home—then, and perhaps only then, the political and social pressures for expanding secondary education will decrease.

The narrowly academic and isolated secondary boarding school soon will have outlived its usefulness and the model for the future may be the early Chavakali. If the function of secondary education becomes less a matter of giving an academic education to young people who will migrate to white-collar jobs in the town and more that of giving a general education to those who will live and work on the land, the secondary school will become more comprehensive and more closely related to its community. Such a school could combine a secondary

---

[7] *After School What? Report of a Joint Working Party of the Christian Council of Kenya and the Christian Churches Educational Association* (Nairobi: 1966), p. 64.

school that gives its students a broad choice of subjects including agriculture, industrial arts, and domestic science, with a community centre that offers adults a broad program that embraces functional literacy classes, the demonstration of farm techniques, and instruction in nutrition and child care. Both by day and evening some of the great promise of educational television might be realized.

Each such school would find its own meaning and purpose, and would evolve differently in the light of the needs and interests of a particular area and the quality of local leadership. But some general predictions could be made. It could combine the high academic standards, the emphasis on service, and the dedication of staff that characterize the Alliance High School tradition with the combined practical and theoretical training and community relationships of Chavakali. By involving secondary school students in the life of the community, by revealing to them that the possession of high intelligence and the satisfactions that come from manual work are not antithetical, and by providing a variety of educative services for adults, this new kind of secondary school could become another agent in hastening a rural transformation.

There appears to be a growing consensus that African primary education also ought to develop more of a rural emphasis.[8] This does not imply teaching vocational agriculture, or using the primary school directly as an agent of community reform. What it can mean is a nurturing within the child of those habits, attitudes, and skills that will prepare him to take part willingly in the agrarian revolution. And as he learns to read, write, and calculate, examples from rural life can be used and the vocabulary and concepts of agriculture introduced. The primary school has the twin objective of helping the young to take root in their village environment but at the same time to accept, indeed to initiate, change. And while the school should

---

[8] See the *Report of the Conference on Education and Scientific and Technical Training in Relation to Development in Africa* sponsored by UNESCO and OAU (Nairobi: July 1968), mimeographed.

give them a pride in their own culture it introduces them to the world outside village and national boundaries. Thus the "ruralizing" of primary education is a much broader and more dynamic concept than teaching agriculture or narrowly adapting education to rural life.

If these are the objectives, how can they be achieved and in what idiom can they be taught? In the New Primary Approach, Kenya has a made-to-order instrument, if she will use it wisely. A primary school method that stresses discovery and exploration, that breaks with bookishness and brings rural life into the classroom, and uses an active and inquiring approach to teaching and learning can provide a means of developing qualities of curiosity and initiative, readiness to cooperate, and tolerance for change that are precisely the qualities that young citizens of a developing country need. But under NPA this is now more the ideal than the reality. Because of the rapid expansion of NPA classes, the lack of texts and materials, the inadequate preparation of teachers, and the shortage of supervisors, the very considerable promise of NPA and all that it stands for in bringing a new spirit and new techniques to primary education is not being realized. At the heart of the problem is the quality of the teacher, and if one phase of primary education seems to cry out more than any other for support and improvement it is teacher training. The needs are many: the recruitment of more trainees with a partial or full secondary education, the continuous upgrading of present staff, and the reform of both the climate and the curriculum of the training colleges. With high urgency Kenya needs primary teachers who can take their place as community leaders of maturity and initiative, who understand the need for rural transformation, and see education as one of the tools for achieving it.

Whatever strategies Kenya employs in reforming and shaping her educational system in the years ahead she will face all the constraints and pressures that define the options and heighten the tensions of a new and developing country. An expanding population and an almost religious faith in education create pressures for expanding school enrollments, while limited resources and a shortage of qualified teachers impose severe constraints. If economic development is to go forward, manpower quotas must be met, but not oversubscribed, and national considerations outweigh individual concerns for growth and development. On the other hand, the educator insists that the objectives of educational planning cannot be confined to economic or political considerations. He wants to improve the quality of education and, certainly, the education and training of teachers. But any large-scale upgrading of teachers' qualifications may result in a salary bill that the country cannot afford to pay.

It is through this complexity of constraints and pressures that Kenya is now finding her way. She is also bringing change and modification to a colonial system of education. In place of a system organized on racial lines and administered by Christian missions the schools are now integrated and have become the instruments of a secular state. And in place of a training for white-collar employment and a vision of the good life derived from Western Europe, the new leaders seek to adapt education to African traditions and African realities.

And thus the wheel comes full circle, for this is Phelps Stokes "adaptation" forty-five years later. But with a difference. The proposals for change are not coming from colonial administrators with reference to the "backward races," and Africans are no longer apprehensive that such proposals are attempts to fob off on them an inferior kind of education. On the contrary, African leaders, including President Kenyatta, have stressed the need for education as a means of improving life in the rural areas, and President Nyerere's parable of the starving village reveals his belief that a developing country needs a responsible élite with its conscience tuned towards the public good:

> Those who receive this privilege [an extended education], therefore, have a duty to repay the sacrifice others have made. They are like the man who has been given all the food avail-

able in a starving village in order that he might have strength to bring supplies back from a distant place. If he takes the food and does not bring help to his brothers, he is a traitor. Similarly, if any of the young men and women who are given an education by the people of the Republic adopt attitudes of superiority, or fail to use their knowledge to help the development of the country, then they are betraying our Union.[9]

Education is, of course, only one of several partners that share the task of quickening the pace of development. Vigorous and imaginative leadership combined with sound and realistic planning; land reform, agricultural research, and settlement schemes; the intelligent use of foreign aid—these are only a few of the factors on which depend the rate and quality of national growth. But among them education has a special role to play. It can identify and train talent and thus hasten economic advance through a high level of technical and managerial competence. It can provide the practical know-how that a small holder needs to move beyond the level of subsistence farming. It can ease the tensions of tribalism and contribute to the development of a national identity. But at a deeper level education can prepare men to find their way with pride and dignity in the new world that political, economic, and scientific change has opened to them.

---

[9] Julius Nyerere, quoted in George Skorov, *Integration of Educational and Economic Planning in Tanzania* (Paris: International Institute for Educational Planning, 1966), p. 40.

# Selected Bibliography

## Books and Articles

1. Beeby, C. E., *The Quality of Education in Developing Countries.* Cambridge, Mass.: Harvard University Press, 1966.
2. Carter, Roger, *The Legal Framework of Educational Planning and Administration in East Africa.* Paris: UNESCO—International Institute for Educational Planning, 1966.
3. Castle, E. B., *Growing Up in East Africa,* London: Oxford University Press, 1966.
4. Cowan, L. Gray; O'Connell, James; and Scanlon, David, G., ed., *Education and Nation-Building in Africa.* New York: Frederick A. Praeger, Inc., 1966.
5. Curtis, Arnold; O'Hagan, Charles; Penn, Daphne; and Malone, Ralph, *The New Peak Reading Course.* Nairobi: Oxford University Press, 1965.
6. Curtis, Arnold; Malone, Ralph; and O'Hagan, Charles, *The Pivot English Course.* Nairobi: Longmans, Green & Co., Ltd., 1965.
7. Evans, P. C. C., "Western Education and Rural Productivity in Tropical Africa," *Africa.* XXXII (October, 1962), pp. 313–323.
8. Hoskins, Lewis, *Final Report to the Agency for International Development by Earlham College.* Chavakali, 1964. (Mimeographed.)
9. Hunter, Guy, *Education for a Developing Region, A Study of East Africa.* London: George Allen and Unwin Ltd., 1963.
10. Hutasoit, Marixius; and Prator, Clifford H., *A Study of the "New Primary Approach" in the Schools of Kenya.* Nairobi: Ford Foundation and Ministry of Education, 1965. (Mimeographed.)
11. Huxley, Elspeth, *White Man's Country: Lord Delamere and*

the Making of Kenya. 2nd ed. London: Chatto and Windus, Ltd., 1953.
12. Mboya, Tom, A Development Strategy for Africa: Problems and Proposals. Nairobi: Government Printer, 1967.
13. Mboya, Tom, Freedom and After. London: André Deutsch, 1963.
14. Nyerere, Julius K., Education for Self-Reliance. Dar es Salaam: Government Printer, 1967.
15. O'Hagan, Charles, "English Medium Teaching in Kenya," Oversea Education. XXXIV (October, 1962), pp. 99–106.
16. Oliver, Roland, The Missionary Factor in East Africa. 2nd ed. London: Longmans, Green & Co., Ltd., 1965.
17. Porter, Arthur T., "Crisis in African Education," East Africa Journal. V (June, 1968), pp. 9–17.
18. Resnick, Idrian N., ed. Tanzania: Revolution by Education. Arusha: Longmans of Tanzania, 1968.
19. Scanlon, David G., ed. Traditions of African Education. New York: Teachers College, Columbia University, 1964.
20. Skorov, George, Integration of Educational and Economic Planning in Tanzania. Paris: UNESCO—International Institute for Educational Planning, 1966.

## Committee, Commission, and Conference Reports

1. Advisory Committee on Native Education in the British Tropical African Dependencies. Education Policy in British Tropical Africa. London: His Majesty's Stationery Office, 1925.
2. African Education in Kenya. "The Beecher Report." Nairobi: Government Printer, 1949.
3. Christian Council of Kenya and The Christian Churches' Educational Association. After School, What? Nairobi: 1966. (Mimeographed)
4. Education, Employment and Rural Development. Report of the Kericho Conference. Edited by James R. Sheffield. Nairobi: East African Publishing House, 1966.
5. Kenya Education Commission Report. "The Ominde Report." Nairobi: Government Printer, Part I, 1964; Part II, 1965.
6. Phelps Stokes Commission. Education in East Africa. New York: Phelps Stokes Fund, 1924.

## Kenya Government Documents

MINISTRY OF AGRICULTURE

1. *Report of the Agricultural Education Commission.* Nairobi: Government Printer, 1967.

MINISTRY OF ECONOMIC PLANNING AND DEVELOPMENT

1. *African Socialism and its Application to Planning in Kenya.* Nairobi: Government Printer, 1965.
2. *Economic Survey.* Nairobi: Government Printer, 1968.
3. *Family Planning in Kenya.* Nairobi: Government Printer, 1967.
4. *High Level Manpower Requirements and Resources in Kenya 1964–70.* Nairobi: Government Printer, 1965.
5. *Kenya Development Plan 1965–70.* Nairobi: Government Printer, 1966.
6. *Three Years of Independence: Building for a Better Future.* Nairobi: Government Printer, 1966.
7. *Towards a Better Future for Our People.* Nairobi: Government Printer, 1966.

MINISTRY OF EDUCATION

1. *Annual Reports and Trienniel Surveys.* Nairobi: Government Printer, 1923–1967.
2. *The Curriculum Development and Research Centre: A Report on its Background, Current Activities and Future Plans.* Nairobi: Government Printer, 1968. (Mimeographed.)
3. *Primary School Syllabus.* Nairobi: Government Printer, 1967.
4. *The Safari Upper Primary English Course.* Nairobi: Curriculum Development and Research Centre, 1967.
5. *Teacher Education Bulletin.* Nairobi: Equatorial Publishers, 1967 and 1968.

MINISTRY OF INFORMATION

1. *Kenya Profile.* Nairobi: Ministry of Information. 1966.